Additional Praise for *The MultiCapital Scorecard*

"In an interdependent world replete with social, ecological, and economic perils, multicapitalism is an idea whose time has come. With a blend of passion, pragmatism, and pedagogy, Thomas and McElroy chart a pathway to transforming a lofty concept into a critical operational tool for enterprise management in the 21st century. Universal adoption promises to fuel a virtuous circle of multicapital enrichment by business that, in turn, will yield long-term systems resilience that undergirds company—and societal—prosperity. This volume, in short, is a roadmap toward a livable world."   —**Allen White**, cofounder and former CEO, Global Reporting Initiative; founder, Global Initiative for Sustainability Ratings

"Thomas and McElroy's emphasis on using context-based metrics is fundamental. Operating without context is like standing on a scale without knowing your ideal weight, tracking your speed without understanding the speed limit, or monitoring your income while ignoring your expenditures. In the same way, the sustainability performance of organizations needs to be tracked relative to limits and thresholds in the world, as clearly illustrated by the MultiCapital Scorecard. This is why *The MultiCapital Scorecard* originates a whole new generation of triple bottom line accounting."—**Mathis Wackernagel**, founder and CEO, Global Footprint Network

"In order for sustainability reporting to provide an accurate picture of a company's impact on the economy, environment, and the society in which it operates, context must be given to the reported information. While the context principle was introduced in 2002, it has largely been absent in corporate reporting, partially due to a lack of available guidance on how to apply context to reporting. *The Multicapital Scorecard* is a step forward in addressing this gap and encouraging a widespread dissemination of context-based sustainability reporting."—**Elisa Tonda**, head of the Responsible Industry and Value Chain Unit, UNEP

"*The MultiCapital Scorecard* provides a valuable aid to help companies get to grips with the complex set of resources and relationships upon which all organizations impact and depend. The context-based approach is a particularly important development, as social and environmental issues put ever greater constraints on business and the economy, and provide real opportunities for those providing solutions."   —**Jessica Fries**, executive chairman, the Prince's Accounting for Sustainability Project (A4S)

"*Sustainability* is mainstream practice. *Integration* is a keyword. But if we want these words to be truly meaningful in a management context—and to have the positive impact on planet and people that we all hope for—then we must also face up to some hard facts and tough choices. With this long-overdue dose of conceptual clarity and ethical rigor, Thomas and McElroy help us do that, drawing inspiration from the best of systems science, financial accounting, and other disciplines. This is a must-read book for everyone who is serious about responsible enterprise in the age of sustainable development." **—Alan AtKisson**, coauthor of *Parachuting Cats into Borneo*; president, AtKisson Group

"As anyone in business knows, maintaining capital intact is essential. Running permanent long-term overdrafts is not—it leads to collapse. This book makes it clear that the ultimate source of all value (natural and human capital) is under threat and sets out a series of practical and useful measurement tools that can aid business managers in the necessary turnaround. Measuring and managing an organization's social and environmental impacts is a useful start, but this book goes much further. With its systems-based philosophy and context-based target setting, it offers the kind of transformational thinking so necessary to reorganize business ecologically." **—Markus J. Milne**, professor of accounting, University of Canterbury

"Measuring corporate sustainability performance is unlikely to bring about sustainable change unless we also challenge underlying business models, understand context, and consider ecological and social constraints. The MultiCapital Scorecard is one of the few performance measurement frameworks that attempts to integrate planetary-boundary thinking into everyday management and accounting practices. Without making these limits visible to managers, there is the danger that corporations march themselves and others blindly toward a more unsustainable future." **—Ian Thomson**, professor of accounting and sustainability, University of Birmingham

"This book is a meticulous piece of work, analytically outstanding, detailed, and very worthwhile reading. It is an important next step in multicapital thinking and policy making. Let us hope that many organizations in the future become willing to report in a structured way like this." **—Jo M. L. van Engelen**, chaired professor of integrated sustainable solutions, Delft University of Technology

"Thomas and McElroy have cut through much of the noise and bluster around business and 'sustainability.' They recognize many of the complexities of the issues, and they provide a pragmatically coherent program by which managers might be encouraged to actively begin to address just how their organizations could be tempted toward initial substantive steps away from unsustainability." **—Rob Gray**, coauthor of *Accountability, Social Responsibility and Sustainability*; emeritus professor, University of St. Andrews

The
MultiCapital
Scorecard

Also by Mark W. McElroy

Corporate Sustainability Management:
The Art and Science of Managing Non-Financial Performance,
with Jo M. L. van Engelen

Key Issues in the New Knowledge Management,
with Joseph M. Firestone

The New Knowledge Management:
Complexity, Learning and Sustainable Innovation

"The Social Footprint Method," in *The Sustainability*
Practitioner's Guide to Social Analysis and Assessment,
edited by Joy Murray, Darian McBain, and Thomas Weidmann

"Social Footprints: Measuring the
Social Sustainability Performance of Organizations,"
PhD dissertation, University of Groningen

Also by Martin P. Thomas

"Performance That Lasts: How Leading
Organisations Measure Performance in 2050,"
in *New Eyes: The Human Side of Leadership,*
edited by Joanne Flinn, Roberto Saco,
Mike Staresinic, and Dan Ballbach

"Scenarios Towards Social Dialogue,"
in *Business Planning for Turbulent Times,*
edited by Rafael Ramirez, John W. Selsky,
and Kees van der Heijden

The
MultiCapital
Scorecard

RETHINKING
ORGANIZATIONAL
PERFORMANCE

Martin P. Thomas and Mark W. McElroy

Foreword by Sir Ian Cheshire

Chelsea Green Publishing
White River Junction, Vermont

Editor: Joni Praded
Project Manager: Alexander Bullett
Copy Editor: Deborah Heimann
Proofreader: Eric Raetz
Indexer: Shana Milkie
Designer: Melissa Jacobson

Printed in the United States of America.
First printing November, 2016.
10 9 8 7 6 5 4 3 2 1   16 17 18 19 20

Chelsea Green Publishing is committed to preserving
ancient forests and natural resources. We elected to
print this title on paper containing at least 10% postconsumer recycled paper, processed chlorine-free. As a
result, for this printing, we have saved:

8 Trees (40' tall and 6-8" diameter)
3,650 Gallons of Wastewater
3 million BTUs Total Energy
245 Pounds of Solid Waste
673 Pounds of Greenhouse Gases

Chelsea Green Publishing made this paper choice
because we are a member of the Green Press Initiative,
a nonprofit program dedicated to supporting authors,
publishers, and suppliers in their efforts to reduce their
use of fiber obtained from endangered forests. For
more information, visit www.greenpressinitiative.org.

Environmental impact estimates were made using the
Environmental Defense Paper Calculator. For more
information visit: www.papercalculator.org.

Our Commitment to Green Publishing

Chelsea Green sees publishing as a tool for cultural change and ecological stewardship. We strive to align our book
manufacturing practices with our editorial mission and to reduce the impact of our business enterprise in the environment. We print our books and catalogs on chlorine-free recycled paper, using vegetable-based inks whenever possible.
This book may cost slightly more because it was printed on paper that contains recycled fiber, and we hope you'll agree
that it's worth it. Chelsea Green is a member of the Green Press Initiative (www.greenpressinitiative.org), a nonprofit
coalition of publishers, manufacturers, and authors working to protect the world's endangered forests and conserve
natural resources. *The MultiCapital Scorecard* was printed on paper supplied by LSC Communications that contains at
least 10% postconsumer recycled fiber.

Library of Congress Cataloging-in-Publication Data

Names: Thomas, Martin P., 1946- author. | McElroy, Mark W., author.
Title: The multicapital scorecard : rethinking organizational performance /
   Martin P. Thomas and Mark W. McElroy.
Description: White River Junction, Vermont : Chelsea Green Publishing, [2016]
   | Includes bibliographical references and index.
Identifiers: LCCN 2016032364| ISBN 9781603586900 (hardcover) | ISBN
   9781603586917 (ebook)
Subjects: LCSH: Sustainable development reporting. |
   Management--Environmental aspects. | Benchmarking (Management)
Classification: LCC HD60.3 .T46 2016 | DDC 658.4/083--dc23
LC record available at https://lccn.loc.gov/2016032364

Chelsea Green Publishing
85 North Main Street, Suite 120
White River Junction, VT 05001
(802) 295-6300
www.chelseagreen.com

MIX
Paper from
responsible sources
FSC® C132124

*We dedicate this book
to two friends who inspired its writing.
For Martin, it was the late Clive Emmanuel, whose
encouragement of unconventional thinking was legendary.
For Mark, it was Joseph Firestone, whose teachings on
Popperian epistemology, truth, and value theory were liberating.
We honor you both and hope our work
does justice to your principles.*

CONTENTS

FOREWORD

I have been involved in the world of corporate social responsibility and sustainability for nearly two decades, both as group chief executive of Kingfisher plc, the international retailer, and also through the Cambridge Institute for Sustainability Leadership, as chair of their advisory board. Beyond this I have been involved with a number of campaigning groups, such as Business in the Community and Accounting for Sustainability.

In my experience, most modern corporate leaders understand the need to ensure our business models are truly sustainable. We know that sustainability must be a core part of overall strategy, not just an afterthought. We recognize that we are currently working inside a system that, by 2030, will consume two planets' worth of resources, but (when we last looked!) we only have one to work with. We will need to transform the way our economy works so that we can understand how our businesses use all forms of capital—natural, human, and financial—in productive and sustainable ways.

The difficulty for most of us lies not in convincing our teams of that logic but in planning and measuring our progress so that we can make the change actually happen. We have seen hundreds of years of practice in double-entry bookkeeping and can measure financial capital to the nth degree, but we lack the tools to describe our businesses and their impact in terms of natural or human capital, which are also often highly complex issues. However, we should be trying to develop such tools, even if they are unlikely to be perfect from the outset.

The MultiCapital Scorecard

Many initiatives are underway, but I particularly welcome the Multi-Capital Scorecard as a coherent attempt to provide a practical scorecard tool that teams across businesses can use to set goals and measure progress. It is especially important that people at all levels have a common metric and approach that allows leadership to happen at all points in an organization. As the scorecard becomes used more widely, I am sure we will learn how to develop further elements and metrics, but it gives us a great start, and in this field the perfect is often the enemy of the good.

The MultiCapital Scorecard framework is designed around principles and so can be scaled up to fit any model and adjusted to fit the differing impacts on society, the environment, and the economy that each business or other type of organization generates. I strongly believe that each organization needs to understand its unique impacts in order to seize its opportunity to create value sustainably. There is no simple, generic strategy that does this in all contexts.

Ultimately, what makes the MultiCapital Scorecard so potentially valuable for all of us is that, by measuring our impacts and progress, we will unleash the power of our teams to do more. What gets measured gets done! I congratulate Martin Thomas and Mark McElroy for their work and recommend it to you.

SIR IAN CHESHIRE
London
June 2016

ACKNOWLEDGMENTS

We both have to think back several decades to acknowledge the people and organizations who formed our values and fundamental knowledge. Unilever, with its long history of an enlightened management ethos, trained and formed Martin. ICSA: The Governance Institute awarded him its postgraduate exhibition that funded his masters in financial control in the early years of Lancaster University's business school. Professors Clive Emmanuel, Eddie Stamp, John Perrin, and Roger Fawthrop were all instrumental in broadening Martin's ideas of what accounting and performance measurement could become. Henk Meij was instrumental in allowing some of those ideas to flourish in Unilever.

The University of Oxford and HEC Paris Consulting and Coaching for Change MSc of 2003–2004 was instrumental in bringing together and shaping the human catalysts for change (like Martin) who in 2005 became the Change Leaders. They all benefited from the ideas of Chris Argyris, Richard Pascale, Rafael Ramirez, Elizabeth Howard, Denis Bourgeois, and others. From this cohort emerged New Angles, a Paris-based consulting practice with a clear focus on supporting change initiatives toward sustainable futures. Jacob Mayne, Mick Yates, Wessel Pretorius, and Margareta Barchan were all critical in sharpening Martin's work toward producing a viable process for sustainability performance measurement.

Mark's entry into the field of sustainability was ushered in by no less that Donella (Dana) Meadows, with whom he had the great pleasure to work and collaborate at her Sustainability Institute in Vermont starting in the mid-nineties and continuing until her untimely death in 2001, when he was chair of the board there. Mark would go on to pursue his shared interest with Dana in metrics and indicators for sustainability and sustainable development, culminating in his doctoral dissertation on the subject in 2008 at the University of Groningen. He will forever be grateful for the guidance and support he received from his supervisors there, Professors Jo M. L. van Engelen, the late René J. Jorna, and D. J. Kiewiet.

Mark also wishes to acknowledge and thank the good folks at Schumacher College in Dartington, Devon, England who in 1997 provided him with a solid foundation in Gaia Theory, arguably the quintessential systems theory of natural capital on Earth. Special thanks, in particular, go to Stephan Harding and James Lovelock in this regard.

Also important to Mark's intellectual development and the ideas put forward in this book have been Joseph M. Firestone and Steven A. Cavaleri, whose tutelage in epistemology, organizational learning, and clear thinking indelibly changed his life.

The Centre for Social and Environmental Accounting Research (CSEAR) at University of St. Andrews provided the crucible in which Mark's and Martin's ideas first came together in 2011. The encouragement and support of many CSEAR members have been important in the drafting of this book. Particularly deserving of mention are Professors Ian Thomson, Jan Bebbington, Rob Gray, and Mike Jones. Comments on various drafts of the book have been welcomed from many quarters. A most thorough review was conducted by Mark Evens: His candid observations contributed to many improvements. He also developed some more sophisticated data collection and scoring ideas that could be applied to the National Health Service (in addition to the MultiCapital Scorecard®* as we have described it in this book). Professor Stefan Schaltegger also offered helpful guidance and encouragement. Ian Thomas provided critical support in setting out the

---

* The name *MultiCapital Scorecard* is trademarked in the United States and other parts of the world. The underlying methodology, however, is open-source and free for the taking by organizations for end-user applications. Third party use, however, by consultancies or others in the delivery of professional services is prohibited without permission from Thomas & McElroy LLC and may be subject to licensing requirements.

worked examples at the heart of this book. Thanks to Larry Hirschhorn, Gill Ringland, Barbara Heinzen, Hardin Tibbs, and Sara Newmark for their intellectual inputs, too.

Special thanks also go out to Rob Michalak and Jostein Solheim of Ben & Jerry's Homemade (a subsidiary of Unilever), global director of social mission and CEO, respectively, and Jed Davis, director of sustainability at Cabot Creamery Cooperative, for their pioneering spirits in helping us to test, evaluate, and improve the MultiCapital Scorecard in its early days. We and it are all the better off because of it.

We would also like to thank Joni Praded and the team at Chelsea Green for their hard work and supportive approach, converting our manuscript into the book you have in your hands.

Our wives, too, have had to bear the brunt of holidays, evenings, and weekends in which the MultiCapital Scorecard has had priority over all else. Our sincere thanks therefore go to Theresa Thomas and Amy McElroy for their unwavering support.

Despite all the help and influences acknowledged above, we recognize there will inevitably be many errors and shortcomings in this book. We take full responsibility for them all. We also hope that potential adopters of the MultiCapital Scorecard will not feel themselves constrained by a need for perfection. The world calls on us all to do our best to protect, preserve, and grow our natural, human, social, and other capitals while creating economic value. In this, we consider the search for perfection to be a counsel of despair. Why? Because as Dana Meadows once said, "it is important to get some preliminary indicators out there and into use, the best we can do at the moment." Much good learning comes from doing. Meanwhile, precious time is a-wasting!

Introduction

We, the authors, have grown up and earned our living in a western world shaped essentially by capitalism. That has traditionally meant the generation of economic capital, mainly for the benefit of shareholders or other providers of financial capital. We understand the powerful driving forces that underlie such a purpose. We acknowledge the contribution that economic capitalism has made to the industrial revolution, social structures, and the development of many of the technologies on which the world has come to depend.

However, we also recognize the enormity of the environmental footprint our economic growth has left over the last 250 years and the ever-growing disparity between that footprint's annual demands and the biosphere's capacity to support them. We believe that these ecological issues cannot be resolved without addressing the intergenerational deficit we are creating and the gap that today exists between the world's wealthiest two billion inhabitants and its poorest two billion.

We therefore believe the world needs to attend to the quality and sufficiency of all its vital capitals, not just its economic capitals. This is what we call **multicapitalism**. It is a doctrine that measures and manages impacts organizations are having on multiple capitals and therefore their own **triple bottom lines**: their social, environmental, and economic performance.[1]

Although many noteworthy institutions accept the validity of the need to preserve multiple capitals, we have yet to see any principles or practices that enable organizations to enact multicapitalism in a meaningful way. Hence this book.

1

The MultiCapital Scorecard

The principles underpinning our approach to multicapitalism are those of Context-Based Sustainability. They owe their heritage to one of us, Mark McElroy, and Jo van Engelen, as set forth in their book, *Corporate Sustainability Management*, in 2012.[2] That book dealt with nonfinancial performance drawing on stakeholder engagement; this book deals with performance impacting all capitals, including financial capital. It applies identical principles to engagement with all vital stakeholders.

McElroy and Van Engelen's 2012 book gave pioneering worked examples of Context-Based Sustainability in practice. Those examples illustrated how groundbreaking projects set thresholds for sustainable performance for social and environmental impacts in their appropriate contexts. We have adopted in this book the practices set out by McElroy and Van Engelen, while extending them to embrace financial and economic capitals as well.

The result is a "multiple capitals" approach to management that, for the first time, offers organizations of all sorts a triple bottom line performance measurement model that can indicate how far an organization is from performing sustainably. It can be used to measure progress toward sustainability, too. We do not pretend that this approach can provide a perfect measurement initially, but we do believe it offers a meaningful learning framework. While the learning proceeds, the MultiCapital Scorecard provides the best method available for measuring performances impacting all capitals—financial, social, natural, and more—using identical evaluation principles for them all. Performance is reported against context-based sustainability norms, science-based and otherwise. Consequently, organizations of all sorts adopting the MultiCapital Scorecard are able to see for the first time the extent to which their impacts on all vital capitals are sustainable, set target thresholds, and monitor progress toward meeting them.

Indeed, measuring shortfalls and surpluses against sustainability thresholds across multiple capitals is an entirely new concept, and it offers an entirely new way to manage performance. The very act of providing routine scorecard results will initiate paradigm shifts in most of the organizations that adopt it. As they use their historic performance data to improve future performance, the old paradigm of maximizing impact on a single capital will gradually give way to recognizing the need to manage impacts on multiple capitals.

Introduction

Since the objectives of many stakeholder groups are in conflict with each other at any given organization, there will be many cases where directors, governors, owners, and managers will have to decide on allocating scarce resources between competing demands. No simple formula can exist for deciding such allocations. But it is always the case that local context and stakeholder engagement are required inputs to any such responsible decision-making process. Our multicapitalism process provides both in an even-handed manner. Strategic decision takers are therefore presented for the very first time with context-based information about the extent to which their organizations are either fulfilling their duties and obligations or failing to do so.

All the evidence we have seen suggests that most organizations are currently operating in an unsustainable manner. Consequently, it might be seen as a source of embarrassment to report unsustainability to stakeholders. However, we believe the world needs to know the truth (however unpalatable that may be) rather than persisting in willful ignorance of reality. And the call for corporations and other organizations to be responsible and transparent is growing louder. Rating agencies are now rising to this challenge, too, and so must organizations themselves.

Some might argue that in an essentially unsustainable world, it is folly to attempt to assess how an individual organization can reach sustainability on its own. But the application of "fair shares" of available multicapital resources or of the burdens to produce them can provide us with very meaningful reference points to move toward the required collective objective of sustainable futures. Indeed, the basic analysis needed to establish the thresholds of sustainable performance should be a fundamental precursor to any improvement process.

Others might criticize our multicapital performance measurements for their imprecision or subjectivity. To these critics, we ask the question: "Is it better to be precisely wrong or approximately right?" We believe the world needs us all to ask the right questions and for organizations to provide the best information available. Awaiting perfection is a counsel of despair.[3]

Indeed, humanity has a moral duty to safeguard the quality and sufficiency of all vital capitals, the disregard of which is irresponsible. Hiding unethical practice behind a façade of spuriously objective accuracy, while propagating an endless stream of negative externalities, is inexcusable. This is what we call "precisely wrong."

PART ONE

The Dawning of Multicapitalism

CHAPTER ONE

An Overview of the MultiCapital Scorecard

This is a book about a new methodology that organizations can use to measure, manage, and report their performance. It is unlike any other method that has come before it, in that it makes triple bottom line management possible. The method we are referring to, of course, is the MultiCapital Scorecard.

To fully understand and appreciate the MultiCapital Scorecard, one must also understand that it is an extension of what is otherwise known as Context-Based Sustainability. Whereas Context-Based Sustainability was originally conceived as a methodology for assessing the social and environmental performance of organizations, the MultiCapital Scorecard adds economic performance to the mix and thereby qualifies as a fully operationalized triple bottom line method—the first of its kind.

What really differentiates Context-Based Sustainability and the MultiCapital Scorecard from the rest of the field more than anything else, though, is the manner in which they assess performance relative to sustainability thresholds, or what we call *sustainability norms*. A **sustainability norm** is a standard of performance for what an organization's social, environmental, or economic impacts would have to be in order to be sustainable. Here it is important to understand that the MultiCapital Scorecard adopts an interpretation of

Context-Based Sustainability

Context-Based Sustainability is a compelling new approach to sustainability measurement and reporting that takes science- and ethics-based social and environmental limits in the world (upper and lower ones) explicitly into account when attempting to assess the performance of organizations. In order for an organization's use of, or impacts on, natural resources, for example, to be sustainable, it must put neither the sufficiency of such resources nor the well-being of those who depend on them at risk. Rather, it should live within its fair, just, and proportionate shares of ecological means.

Further, since many of the resources involved are shared, Context-Based Sustainability also makes it possible to assign equitable shares of a population's entitlements to consume, or their responsibility to produce and maintain, them to specific organizations. (See appendix D for guidance on how to do this.) Sustainability performance can then be measured relative to organization-specific norms or standards in an organization's own context.

performance that is grounded in sustainability as a regulative ideal. In other words, in the MultiCapital Scorecard, we define performance in terms of sustainability, including financial performance. What makes performance favorable or not, that is, is whether or not it is sustainable, be it social, environmental, or financial performance. Thus, it is the *ideal* of sustainability that we believe should systematically *regulate* our understanding and assessments of organizational performance in *all* of its dimensions.

Performance under the MultiCapital Scorecard is further interpreted in terms of what an organization's impacts on vital capitals are. Like most who hold to such capital-based interpretations of performance, the MultiCapital Scorecard specifically assesses impacts on five vital capitals: natural, human, social and relationship, constructed (including human-built infrastructure),

An Overview of the MultiCapital Scorecard

Originally developed by McElroy at the Center for Sustainable Organizations as a way of narrowly addressing the nonfinancial performance of organizations, Context-Based Sustainability is now being applied to economic and financial performance as well (by Thomas and McElroy), thereby resulting in the MultiCapital Scorecard. In so doing, the same principle of assessing performance relative to limits is applied, albeit to limits on economic resources in the case of financial performance (for example, in the form of floors, or lower limits, for returns on equity).

Of particular importance to both Context-Based Sustainability and the MultiCapital Scorecard is the concept of *carrying capacity*— the size of the load or degree of demand a resource can support without degrading—and the idea that the carrying capacities of vital resources (capitals) must be maintained at desired levels in order to ensure stakeholder or human well-being—anything less is unsustainable. It is the effects an organization's activities have on the carrying capacities of vital capitals relative to norms or limits (and the well-being of stakeholders who depend on them) that determine whether or not its activities are sustainable.

and economic. It also recognizes a sixth capital that may or may not be embedded in the other five: intellectual. These vital capitals are all discussed in further detail in chapter 2, but for now it's important to know that the MultiCapital Scorecard is distinctively capital-based.[1]

In use, the MultiCapital Scorecard is a methodology for measuring, managing, and reporting the performance of organizations, quantifying (a) what their impacts on vital capitals are and (b) how such impacts compare to sustainability norms—the standards for sustainable operations. All such norms are entity-specific and may reach beyond what is legally required. They are defined and adopted by firms themselves, either because of their own missions or by reference to science, ethics, or normative dictates of one sort or another.

The MultiCapital Scorecard

To understand the MultiCapital Scorecard, it is important to understand the distinction we make between capital thresholds and allocations when defining sustainability norms. A **threshold** consists of the carrying capacity of a vital capital, such as the amount of renewable water in a watershed and the size of the population it can support. An **allocation**, in turn, consists of a fair, just, and proportionate share of such thresholds to individual actors. So, in the case of natural capital, allocations would represent an organization's fair, just, and proportionate shares of available natural resources. For other capitals, allocations would represent the organization's fair shares of the burden to continually produce and maintain the components of those capitals—from human labor, skills, and knowledge to social networks, infrastructure, revenue streams, intellectual property, and beyond. Exactly how to calculate such thresholds and allocations across a broad range of social, environmental, and economic capitals in a structured, nonarbitrary way is one of the distinguishing characteristics of the MultiCapital Scorecard.

It is also important to understand that the MultiCapital Scorecard is stakeholder-centric. It assesses how impacts on vital capitals might affect the economic well-being of its shareholders, but, as a triple bottom line methodology, it assesses how those impacts might affect the economic and noneconomic well-being of its other stakeholders, too. It is in this sense that we can say the MultiCapital Scorecard is a creature of multicapitalism—a performance measurement system that does not accord primacy to only one type of capital (economic) at the expense of others. That is, the MultiCapital Scorecard essentially renounces monocapitalism as the basis of performance accounting and replaces it with multicapitalism, hence its name.

It should also be understood that the MultiCapital Scorecard is not a system that relies on monetizing impacts on vital capitals as a way of somehow computing a financial triple bottom line. It could certainly be used in support of such a system, but that is not its aim. Rather, the MultiCapital Scorecard expresses performance on a scale of its own and always by reference to what an organization's impacts on vital capitals would have to be in order to be sustainable (that is, in accordance with the sustainability norms it has defined for itself).

Next, we feel compelled to point out that Context-Based Sustainability itself and the MultiCapital Scorecard expansion of it described in this book took much of their inspiration from the long history of financial measurement and reporting. Indeed, financial accounting has been nothing if not stakeholder- and capital-based from the start, albeit with respect to only one stakeholder group (shareholders) and one type of capital (economic). Still, mainstream financial management is fully grounded in sustainability norms of its own and always has been: Economic capital should be maintained at levels that do not erode the opening balances of shareholders' funds. The MultiCapital Scorecard merely takes the same idea and extends it to the other capitals, while recognizing other stakeholders, other capital impacts, and other sustainability norms.

When all is said and done, the MultiCapital Scorecard is a tool for answering two basic questions in performance accounting: How much is enough when it comes to consuming or producing capitals? And are our activities and operations sustainable? This is the essence of triple bottom line, multiple capital accounting.

In the process of answering these questions, the MultiCapital Scorecard provides a framework that functions as a moral compass. By engaging systematically with stakeholders and listening to their views on the organization's moral and ethical duties, management, leaders, and all those charged with governance can make judgments about what they stand for and which claims of stakeholders they choose to accept or not to accept. Openly and transparently, their positions can be stated and acted on.

Never was the need for such a process more clearly demonstrated than by the Panama Papers leaks revealed in April 2016.[2] The age of transparency swept in with tsunami-sized waves. Organizations using legality and nondisclosure as their only lines of defense saw their leadership washed away in a matter of days. Establishing moral and ethical norms is now clearly an essential part of doing business of all sorts for organizations of all kinds. It is no longer acceptable to profess that a company or other institution has no moral or ethical duties beyond legal requirements. We the authors wholeheartedly endorse the view that duties may transcend the minimum standards mandated by law and offer the MultiCapital Scorecard as an "open source" process, free for all to use. The moral compass that starts as a by-product of triple bottom line, integrated thinking should itself become the beating heart of the sustainable organization.

Why We Need the MultiCapital Scorecard

Leaders ask why. Why commit time, money, and people to a project without which we have lived for generations? We offer eight reasons why organizations need qualitative improvements to survive the coming decades:

1. New challenges: environmental and social
2. Adaptive capacity
3. Stakeholder engagement
4. Evolving norms
5. Meaningful management information
6. Organizational learning
7. Reputations
8. Integrated reporting

New Challenges: Environmental and Social

There is only one planet Earth and humankind is placing too great a demand on its natural resources already (see figure 1.1). Despite knowing this for at least the last twenty years, humankind has failed to curb these excess demands. Leaders attentive to the needs of the world ask whether their own organization may have a responsibility to address this issue. They also ask how the natural boundaries of resource availabilities and climate change may affect their organizations. Furthermore, they ask how they set about balancing the needs of the planet with the needs of the people on the planet and with their own organization's economic needs.

This book cannot answer these questions with respect to any particular organization, of course, but it does offer the only approach we know to finding the answers for every organization in its own context. We treat impacts on natural, human, social, and constructed capitals in the same ways we do economic capital. We consider all of them to be inextricably interconnected. Each deserves its own due attention, as do the links between them.

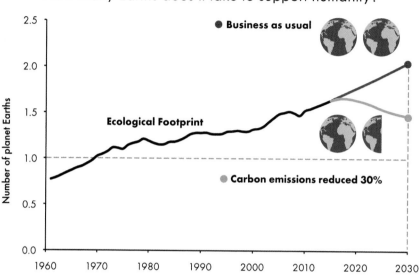

Figure 1.1. Global ecological footprint. On our current "business as usual" trajectory, we would need 2 planet Earths for humanity's current rate of consumption to be sustainable by 2030. And even with a reduction in carbon emissions of 30 percent by the same date, we would need roughly 1.4 planet Earths. Image copyright © 2016 Global Footprint Network. For more information, see http://www.footprintnetwork.org.

The concept of overall sustainability is moving out of its prior niche and into the mainstream, and as it does, corporate and other leaders need to take stock of their operations. If leaders seek the answers seriously and discover that they are fulfilling their duties to all stakeholders and have no responsibility to alter their existing practices, they have acted responsibly. If they fail to ask the questions or refuse to seek the real answers, they have acted irresponsibly—like gamblers playing Russian roulette, but with the lives of distant populations and of future generations in their hands. History will probably judge them accordingly.

Adaptive Capacity

Turbulent times require businesses and other organizations to adapt to new and constantly emerging conditions.[3] Turbulence gives rise to unpredictable change. The nature of the playing field changes and new rules of the game emerge. (See appendix A for a view of how turbulence develops.) The straight lines of planned change are inadequate to deal with such complex realities. The ability to adapt is therefore a vital capability for survival and prosperity. Louisiana State University professor Leon C. Megginson put it this way in his 1963 speech on Charles Darwin's *The Origin of Species*:

> . . . *change is the basic law of nature. But the changes wrought by the passage of time affects individuals and institutions in different ways. According to Darwin's* Origin of Species, *it is not the most intellectual of the species that survives; it is not the strongest that survives; but the species that survives is the one that is able best to adapt and adjust to the changing environment in which it finds itself. Applying this theoretical concept to us as individuals [and organizations, too], we can state that the civilization that is able to survive is the one that is able to adapt to the changing physical, social, political, moral, and spiritual environment in which it finds itself.*[4]

Organizations that do not survive obviously fail all of their stakeholders forever. The ability to adapt relentlessly does not come naturally to many people or organizations, but it can be developed. One characteristic of all adaptive organisms is their constant perception of their context. How else can they prepare themselves for change? But how many organizations actively develop such skills and habits?

Leaders seeking to grow adaptive capacity as an organizational trait need to draw on all the ears, eyes, and data sources at their disposal. It is our belief that an insular focus on the introspective ways of running organizations is tantamount to destroying adaptive capacity. This book offers pathways to building links to both the inside and outside worlds for organizations of all sorts. We ask organizations to draw back the curtains and pull up the blinds to ensure that all can see what is around; open the windows and listen attentively so that everyone can hear what is happening around the world. Anything less undermines the adaptive capacity of a firm and places it on the road to extinction.

We propose a set of principles (together with ways of making them operational) that build performance norms based on the organization's context. Figure 1.2 shows how this systematically incorporates context into the responsive organization. (See appendix B, as well, for a recommended policy model for how to construct a sustainable learning environment.)

Stakeholder Engagement

We define an organization's stakeholders as anyone to whom the organization owes a duty or obligation to manage its impacts on vital capitals in ways that can affect their well-being. This typically includes owners, shareholders, employees, customers, consumers, suppliers, and communities, but all are liable to vary by organization. Identifying stakeholders also requires that we consider future generations and their needs as we contemplate and manage the effects we have on vital capitals today.

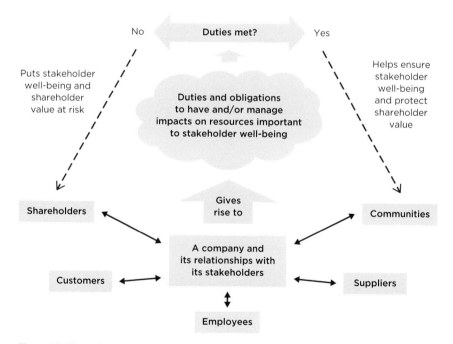

Figure 1.2. The stakeholder- and context-based case for multicapitalism. It is the relationships organizations have with their stakeholders in their own contexts that give rise to duties and obligations to manage their impacts on vital capitals in ways that can affect their (stakeholder) well-being. Adapted from "Clarifying the Business Case for Sustainability and CSR" by Mark W. McElroy, http://www.sustainablebrands.com/news_and _views/articles/clarifying-business-case-sustainability-and-csr.

We propose listening to stakeholders and understanding their concerns as well as their views on what duties and obligations the organization owes them. Duties differ from obligations in the sense that they are only morally or ethically owed, whereas obligations are legally owed, either by law or because of contracts or agreements people have willingly entered into.[5]

Many readers will say that their organizations are already listening to their stakeholders, particularly consumers, customers, and employees. But we extend that net more widely and we propose some mechanisms for collective listening and for dealing with what all stakeholders say.

This is not to say that we believe businesses or other organizations carry the burden of correcting all the wrongs of the world. Indeed, they do not. Instead, our process asks each organization to bear only its fair and proportionate share of responsibilities to achieve and maintain sustainability.

That said, it is also the case that stakeholders' interests will sometimes, if not routinely, be in opposition to each other. But research suggests that leaders should listen to all such groups. We also propose a mechanism for organizations to balance the demands of all stakeholder groups on the basis of comparable information. This enables leaders to explore the impacts of alternative strategies on various capitals and to choose trade-offs between them based on comparable information. Again, we believe this to be a first.

Evolving Norms

In turbulent times, it becomes clear to perceptive leaders that the standards of performance of yesteryear are no longer acceptable. Take as an example the financial services sector in which many participants thought that after the crisis of 2007–2008, "business as usual" would return. Some organizations continued to ignore the call for change. But by 2014 it had become clear to all that society was demanding new norms.

Turbulence theory suggests that organizations should embrace the constant need to attune their own standards of performance to the needs of all their stakeholders. This book offers a means of doing so as a routine business activity. Indeed, the MultiCapital Scorecard is the only process we know of that asks organizations to set sustainability performance standards. Related norms are made explicit and subjected to periodic review. Regardless of the

Two Steps Toward Adopting New Norms and One Step Back

On December 31, 2013, the *Guardian* ran an online piece titled "Barclays Boss Admits It Could Take 10 Years to Rebuild Public Trust."[6] What it referred to, of course, was the damage done by Barclays's involvement in then-recent banking upheavals, including the Libor scandal that erupted when news broke that major banks had manipulated interest rates for their own profit—particularly unsettling as Libor rates set the standard for hundreds of trillions of dollars of loans worldwide. It is worth sharing a passage from the *Guardian* piece here, to underscore the role that new norms play in the lives of corporations and their leaders:

Antony Jenkins said the series of scandals that have rocked the banking system, including the mis-selling of payment protection insurance and Libor fixing, had damaged the bank's reputation over the long term. "Trust is a very easy thing to lose, and a very hard thing to win back. In my view it will take several years—probably five to ten—to rebuild trust in Barclays," he said. "I can only be responsible for Barclays but I'm hoping in what we do at Barclays we can also rebuild trust in banking."

During the conversation the Barclays boss said he was setting his bank a target of being more trusted than not by 2018, the reverse of which is true now according to the bank's own research.

Jenkins, who was appointed chief executive in August 2012 after his predecessor was forced to step down over the bank's role in the Libor scandal, expressed frustration that too much emphasis is placed on short-term factors such as share prices.

As an ironic footnote, the *Financial Times* reported on July 13, 2015, that Jenkins was sacked in favor of a successor who would have "the ability to put plans in place that deliver shareholder value." New norms do not necessarily evolve in a linear fashion.

sustainability agenda, aligning performance norms to the needs of stake-holders is no simple matter, and the MultiCapital Scorecard offers a practical solution for how to perform this essential management task.

Meaningful Management Information

The MultiCapital Scorecard has been designed for organizations that seek to improve their own performance. Such organizations need to provide the best information possible to make the tough decisions about how to deploy scarce resources toward reducing unsustainable behavior. The infor-mation therefore needs to be relevant to all decision makers. It needs to be meaningful at the local level of an operating company, division, or branch. But it also needs to produce meaningful information for global leaders of divisionalized organizations, the CEOs of multinational companies, and leaders of NGOs. The MultiCapital Scorecard draws on local context, incorporates global norms for global impacts, and offers a consolidation process for linking the two in ways that are meaningful to leaders at all levels. Making more meaning can be called learning. The MultiCapital Scorecard is the best framework we know to encourage organizations to constantly improve their procedures and norms to understand how best to reduce their unsustainable performance.

Make no mistake, this is completely different from processes designed to improve comparability between reporting entities solely to facilitate financial investors' decisions. Performance indicators that take no account of context are often meaningless. Comparing meaningless data sets can confer no more meaning. It only adds cost and administrative work. Beware, therefore, of all "disclosure" initiatives that require data that means nothing to the people preparing it or to those who are using it.

The developers of the Natural Capital Protocol seem to agree. In their draft protocol dated November 23, 2015, they emphasize the importance of meaningful data from management accounting as follows:

There are obvious parallels between the protocol and management account-ing. Disclosure through reporting can be an important driver as well, but it needs to be introduced at the right time. An early push for disclosure is

*tempting, but it does not always drive change and can occasionally stimu-
late risk adverse [sic] behavior, rather than push for innovation.*[7]

In other words, the Natural Capital Protocol prefers to develop meaningful performance data from within the reporting organizations rather than to
impose "[a]n early push for disclosure" (external reporting) that could bring
adverse consequences. This is exactly why the MultiCapital Scorecard encourages
the learning processes through seeking meaningful context-based performance
measurement data. Once such practices become commonplace and many commonly held norms emerge, the time may be right to harmonize performance
standards and drive for comparable disclosure through external reporting. This
bottom-up approach differs dramatically from the top-down philosophy characteristic of strong hierarchies that had success in less turbulent times.

Meanwhile, the MultiCapital Scorecard focuses on the detailed local,
regional, and global context of each component of each organization. As
we've said, we do not pretend that this is a simple process. However, we do
argue that providing meaningful information to management is a prerequisite of a sustainable system and that close attention to context is an essential
element of any such process.

Organizational Learning

A learning organization may take a decade or two to work progressively
toward becoming a leader in the field of multiple capital management. There
is no quick fix. The sooner a start is made the better, therefore. However, a false
start can set progress back and create unnecessary or unwarranted resistance
to change. We advocate engaging enthusiasts from within the organization
from across the whole spectrum of its activities. This requires a learning
framework that enables the organization to deal with small steps one at a time.

The purposeful self-renewing organization, described by Gill Ringland
et al. in *Beyond Crisis*, provides a full explanation of how leaders should
encourage innovation: "Their role is not only to develop the leadership tools
in their team, but to create an environment in which innovation can come
from any role in the organization."[8] We believe that this approach is important to engaging the whole organization in its journey toward sustainability.

A Heritage of Social and Environmental Capital Creation

In the late nineteenth century, one of Unilever's founding fathers, William Hesketh Lever, provided houses for his employees to live close to his soap factory in Port Sunlight, Lancashire, United Kingdom. Various architects were commissioned to ensure that the aesthetics of the "village" should create a sense of well-being and community, while avoiding unnecessary uniformity. Public buildings included an art gallery, a cottage hospital, schools, a concert hall, a swimming pool, a church, and a hotel.

This was just one example of Unilever's social capital creations. Another is the cocreation (with the World Wildlife Fund) of the Marine Stewardship Council in the 1990s. Its purpose was and remains to protect global fish stocks and the marine environment in which they thrive. It is therefore a social capital created and maintained to protect an environmental (natural) capital.

More than a century after the construction of Port Sunlight, the relatively new Unilever CEO, Paul Polman, thanked Unilever's UK pensioners for having kept alive through their working lives the ethos of the founders in seeking social and ecological balance in their pursuit of economic capital creation. Unilever's long heritage helped Polman to launch his audacious plan to double the size of the business, while reducing the whole supply chain's adverse socio-ecological impacts in absolute terms. Voted by global sustainability experts consistently from 2011 to 2015 the company most actively committed to sustainability objectives in the world, Unilever worked toward multiple capital objectives long before the idea was invented.[9] Polman unleashed the power from within.

Values that support working toward sustainable futures need to be developed and shared across the field. Yet changes in values are the most difficult of changes to make, touching as they do on issues deeper than culture. Nevertheless, the turbulence literature identifies the need to develop cohesive values in order to manage effectively in turbulent conditions, such as the conditions we find ourselves in today.

When turbulence sets in within and around organizations, command and control management styles fail as managers become remote from the realities on the ground. Effective emerging values are needed to create ethical codes that enable simplified action. Leaders can empower and enable, but they must allow followers to create their own ways of working. Commonly held values therefore become the "power fields" that allow organizations to work effectively in turbulent times. (See appendix A.)

It is of course easier to write a set of espoused values than it is to behave in compliance with them across the organization in everyday work. Nevertheless, it is instructive to see how some forward-thinking leaders of enlightened companies have made efforts to articulate the values they wish to see inculcated into their corporate behaviors. The following quotation from Robert Wood Johnson, one of Johnson & Johnson's founders, predates the "Credo" that has been the company's code of conduct for many decades.

Industry only has the right to succeed where it performs a real economic service and is a true social asset. It is to the enlightened self-interest of modern industry to realize that its service to its customers comes first, its service to its employees and management second, and its service to its stockholders last. It is to the enlightened self-interest of industry to accept and fulfill its share of social responsibility.[10]

Note the "social asset" requirement and the ranking of stakeholder impacts. We do not seek to impose such a ranking on organizations, but we do share the belief that it is to the enlightened self-interest of all organizations to accept and fulfill their shares of social responsibilities. Also note that these values expressed in 1935 are still not shared by many organizations eighty years later.

The MultiCapital Scorecard provides structures, processes, and principles that allow organizations to engage with their stakeholders to understand their contexts better. Building links with key stakeholder groups builds resilience and fosters the development of commonly held values. These shared values are essential to create the effective mechanisms needed to work in decentralized autonomous networks in turbulent times.

The question then arises: "How does an organization go about developing new values and new behaviors from people on every seat in the organization?" In short, it has to empower people throughout the organization to develop and adopt new ways of thinking and new ways of working.

Research findings suggest that values may be changed marginally in the lifetime of an individual, but more radical values changes are seen between different generations: "Fundamental value change takes place gradually; for the most part, it occurs as a younger generation replaces an older one in the adult population of a society."[11] At the level of the organization, therefore, this suggests that its newer cohorts should be engaged in its dialogues around values and their relevance to the needs of society.

However, reflective leaders may be interested to understand the thought patterns by which individuals and groups may process such changes. Researcher Larry Hirschhorn has described such a collective sociopsychodynamic process. (See appendix C.) Typically, a thought or task that enters the system as a routine matter progresses to the authorized, facilitating process: the workflow subsystem. Such routine tasks are then executed via the authorized "rules" for "business as usual," or the normal way of thinking and acting.

However, the task of learning the new ways of thinking needed to work toward eliminating unsustainable behaviors requires specific "legitimate authority" before it can be treated as a development project. Otherwise, the task sits in the inhibiting process, meeting some of the social defenses, such as denial or transference, that prevent the uncertainty from being addressed. Uncertainty that remains unaddressed for long periods of time tends to turn into anxiety, which can be destructive. Tasks that produce new rules to deal with daily life in new ways require the individuals involved to be authorized within a group that is itself authorized to propose those new rules for general adoption.

This explains why the International Integrated Reporting Council (IIRC) finds that the "tone from the top" is what distinguishes successful integrated reporting (commonly referred to as <IR>) implementations from those that fail. Top management needs to grant authority to everyone in the organization to question the status quo and to propose new ways of working. If leaders fail to make this known and in their behavior fail to demonstrate their support for the new ways of thinking and working, the frustration of people within the organization will result in their ideas collecting in the inhibited structure; blocked by perceived lack of authority to articulate or deal with their thoughts and feelings. These principles underpin the processes at the heart of the purposeful self-renewing organization of *Beyond Crisis*.

None of this is to suggest that perfect knowledge or certainty of outcomes can characterize the dialogues around how an organization reduces its unsustainability. Indeed, we can never really know anything with certainty. However, that does not mean that we should do nothing in the face of uncertainty. We have a duty to act toward achieving sustainable futures, basing our action on the best information we can make available.

Consequently, we advise organizations to structure a multiple capital initiative that sets out to explore sustainability norms with explicit authority from the highest level in the organization. It should encourage participation from everyone in the organization who may be keen to contribute. This requires innovative ways of organizing operational work to allow employees to engage in developmental work alongside their operational tasks. A reporting structure should be put into place such that development projects and sustainability norms that need authorization before proceeding to become operational can be approved and the new arrangements publicized fully.

Learning in such new areas of activity will inevitably result in errors. The organization needs to be prepared to accept mistakes, not as career-threatening events, but as integral elements in a process of continuous improvement. A comprehensive policy model for how to construct such a sustainable learning environment is provided in appendix B.

Reputations

As the emissions scandal at Volkswagen (VW) made abundantly clear in late 2015—as if there was ever any doubt—the reputations of firms matter, listed ones in particular, especially when it comes to their market value. Within two weeks of admitting that it had falsified the emissions performance of more than eleven million of its vehicles, Volkswagen's market capitalization had plummeted by roughly 40 percent of its total value, or $34 billion.

From our perspective, Volkswagen's behavior was unsustainable in at least four different ways:

1. It violated the trust of its customers who were misled into thinking the vehicles they purchased performed at a certain level when in fact they did not.
2. It abused the trust of its own employees, most of whom surely would not have had anything to do with the falsification of product specifications, much less misleading customers.
3. It misled regulators, whose responsibilities were to enforce local emissions standards for environmental protection purposes.
4. It obviously put shareholder value at risk to the tune of $34 billion if not more.

All of these violations were in flagrant breach of the company's published code of conduct.[12] That document also describes extensive mechanisms designed to prevent breaches of the code or to raise them internally if staff members suspect breaches may have occurred. This is a warning that the code's paperwork does not constitute the reality of conduct so much as the culture surrounding the code and the behavior of leaders.

When viewed through the lens of a MultiCapital Scorecard, the four impacts above can be seen as indicated in table 1.1.

TABLE 1.1. Sustainability Norms Violated by Volkswagen in 2015

STAKEHOLDER	SUSTAINABILITY NORM	TYPE OF CAPITAL
Customers	Be truthful	Human (ethical entitlements)
Employees	Be truthful	Economic (personal livelihoods)
Regulators	Be truthful	Human (job performance)
Shareholders	Be truthful	Economic (shareholder value)

We would be fully justified, we think, in taking the position that in light of VW's emissions scandal, its corporate social responsibility performance was deficient and that its reputation suffered accordingly. This seems obvious. The decrease in its market capitalization that followed, therefore, can largely be attributed to that. Thus, sustainability performance and the effects it can have on reputation really do matter. They matter not only to the market capitalizations of listed firms and to the shareholders involved, but to the ethos of the whole organization. This clearly impacts all stakeholders' trust in the integrity of the organization as a whole.

Reputation Dividend (RD), a consultancy in the United Kingdom, has built a scientific model linking the reputations of listed firms to their market capitalizations, but with much more than just sustainability performance in mind.[13] At the start of 2015, for example, RD put out a report in which it claimed that at the end of 2014, 17 percent of the S&P 500's market capitalization, or $3.3 trillion, was attributable to corporate reputations.

For individual companies, the contribution can be much higher or lower. Take Apple Inc., for example. Its market capitalization at the end of 2014 was about $647 billion. Even a mere 1 percent increase or decrease in its value would have been about $6.5 billion. And of the $320.3 billion actually attributable to its reputation that year, RD found that at least $26 billion of it, or 4 percent of total market valuation of the company, could be traced to its ongoing sustainability performance alone.[14] That is to say that in the "going concern" business-as-usual mode of operation, RD ascribes 4 percent of the market value of Apple to its social and environmental performance. This is part of the intangible asset called reputation, which is the subject of Apple's Environmental Responsibility and Supplier Responsibility Reports. In line with reports of many other companies, these reports detail progress from year to year, but do not answer any particular question, such as "how much is enough to be sustainable?" Indeed, Apple writes in its 2014 Environmental Responsibility Report:

> *The Office of Environmental Initiatives works with teams across Apple to set strategy, engage stakeholders, and communicate progress. Our integrated approach means that decisions about environmental issues are reviewed at the highest levels of the company.*

But we know we have a long way to go, and a lot of work ahead of us. *And we are committed to increasing openness in our sustainability work.*[15] *(emphasis added)*

Might it be that protection of an intangible asset worth $26 billion would justify adopting the very best processes in the world as soon as possible to provide the best underpinning available to support or enhance the market's perception?

Other companies featured in RD's analysis displayed even higher sustainability (reputation) contributions to value as a percent of market value, including eBay at 8.9 percent, E. I. DuPont at 8.1 percent, and Eli Lilly at 6.9 percent.[16] That's a huge business case for the reputational value of sustainability performance, the likes of which we rarely see or hear about.

And then, of course, the VW case shows us that a failure to act with integrity can also destroy reputations (and their contributions to market value) of all sorts. Once trust in the organization is undermined, the value at risk is the entire equity of the business. Again, reputations matter.

If only for the sake of building market value, then, organizations should take concrete steps to manage and strengthen their reputations, including their sustainability reputations. This is where the MultiCapital Scorecard comes into play. As the only context- and capital-based system for measuring and reporting the sustainability of organizations, there can be no better tool for managing their performance and for building their associated reputations than the MultiCapital Scorecard. No other system defines organization-specific sustainability norms and then measures performance against them as it does; and no other system does all of that relative to the triple bottom line.

Integrated Reporting

Last but not least in the list of requirements for the MultiCapital Scorecard is, of course, the sudden and auspicious appearance of integrated reporting (capital-based integrated reporting). In late 2013, a new international standard was put out by the IIRC known as the Integrated Reporting Framework, or <IR> Framework, for short.[17] The <IR> Framework consists of a set of guidelines for the preparation of corporate reports in which the impacts of organizations on multiple capitals and on their ability to create value are disclosed.

The <IR> Framework is controversial because some believe it does not live up to the vision of integrated reporting earlier put forward in 2009 by the so-called "King III" report, a groundbreaking South African report on corporate governance.[18] In that report, the authors called for a form of reporting that would integrate sustainability- and financial-reporting in a single report. Strictly speaking, the <IR> Framework published in 2013 does not call for that.

Nevertheless, the need for fully fledged integrated reporting continues to grow, since without it there can be no comprehensive disclosure of organizational performance. And on the theory that performance in all of its dimensions calls for an assessment of impacts on all vital capitals relative to sustainability norms, not just some or one of them, only the MultiCapital Scorecard makes that possible at this time.

Importantly, the <IR> Framework does recommend capital-based reporting relative to a multiple capitals model (see figure 1.3), but only

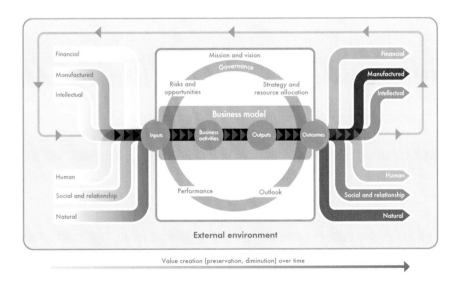

Figure 1.3. IIRC's value creation process with six capitals. The IIRC's "octopus" diagram represents an iterative process with a business model in the center. Six capitals feed in from the left and emerge, transformed, to the right. The business model can create, maintain, or destroy value in any of them, and such value can be financial, nonfinancial, or both. Image courtesy of The International <IR> Framework, http://www.integratedreporting.org.

insofar as impacts on such capitals may affect an organization's ability to create value. Still, we welcome the IIRC's embrace of the multiple capitals view of performance and take the position that the MultiCapital Scorecard more than meets the IIRC's requirements for integrated reporting because it addresses sustainability performance in a comprehensive way. Indeed, the MultiCapital Scorecard may be the only structured methodology that does so at this time.

How to Use This Book

In this first chapter of part 1, we have introduced and explained the need for the MultiCapital Scorecard as being a natural consequence of the new doctrine of multicapitalism first introduced in the introduction. Having done so, we go on in chapter 2 to provide a deeper theoretical foundation for the MultiCapital Scorecard, consisting mainly of a discussion of capital theory and how the MultiCapital Scorecard method qualifies as an extension of Context-Based Sustainability, a sustainability performance accounting system that heretofore did not address financial performance at all. In chapter 2, we also discuss the explicit connections between capital theory and the triple bottom line, a popular metaphor for integrated measurement and reporting that now, with the arrival of the MultiCapital Scorecard, is very much an executable, concrete methodology.

We then continue in chapter 3 with the more practical discussion of how the MultiCapital Scorecard methodology can be put into use. There we include a description of the specific steps practitioners should take to apply the method, and the manner in which organization-specific sustainability norms can be defined as a precursor for measuring, managing, and reporting performance. The mechanics of weighting and scoring performance are also explained.

Next, in chapter 4, we narrowly discuss the extension of Context-Based Sustainability to financial performance, and the necessary treatment of financial and economic capitals that come with it. There we explain how the concept of limits in capitals, already well-established on the social and environmental sides of performance, can be applied to assessments of financial performance as well. Only the types of capitals and the stakeholders involved will differ, even as the same capital-based principles of performance are consistently applied.

In part 2 of the book we provide a very detailed illustration of the Multi-Capital Scorecard in action and the reports it produces. Included therein are reports for three operating units within a fictitious organization, for which performance is measured and reported on both an operating unit and consolidated basis as illustrated in chapters 5 and 6, respectively. The examples we provide otherwise reflect application of the MultiCapital Scorecard in precisely the way explained in chapter 3.

In part 3 of the book we turn our attention to a number of issues raised by the MultiCapital Scorecard and in performance measurement and reporting in general. These include materiality (chapter 7), the treatment of intangibles (chapter 8), and several other key issues, including alternative approaches to integrated reporting (chapter 9).

Part 3 finishes up with chapter 10, in which we present our overall conclusions by focusing on the manner in which the MultiCapital Scorecard helps close gaps between academia and practice, perfection and pragmatism, shareholder and stakeholder primacy, standardization and meaning making, and top-down versus bottom-up action. Finally, a recapitulation of the MultiCapital Scorecard method itself is provided as well.

CHAPTER TWO

Vital Capitals and the MultiCapital Scorecard

Performance measurement in business has largely boiled down to assessing impacts on economic capital with shareholder well-being in mind. That was acceptable so long as the biosphere could support constant economic growth. But now we know we are hitting the global limits of the earth's carrying capacity. The world now also needs to take into account its natural and social capitals if business and other organizations are to prosper. Consequently, we are now entering a new era in which performance assessments will increasingly take the form of measuring impacts on multiple forms of capital with stakeholder well-being in mind. As you've learned in chapter 1, we call this multicapitalism, a new economic doctrine that assesses organizational performance in terms of impacts on all vital capitals, not just one of them.

What Is Capital?

For our purposes, we adopt a definition of capital that follows from those of many others:[1]

Capital is a stock of anything that yields a flow of valuable goods or services important for human well-being.

Here we hasten to add that from our perspective, the sufficiency of vital capitals for nonhuman well-being—natural capital, in particular—is, too, vitally important for human well-being. Because of that, we see nothing unduly anthropocentric in our definition.

On the extension of the term *capital* from its original economic context to the broader one we cite above, ecological economists Robert Costanza and Herman Daly had this to say:

Since "capital" is traditionally defined as produced (manufactured) means of production, the term "natural capital" needs explanation. It is based on a more functional definition of capital as "a stock that yields a flow of valuable goods and services into the future." What is functionally important is the relation of a stock yielding a flow; whether the stock is manufactured or natural is in this view a distinction between kinds of capital and not a defining characteristic of capital itself.[2]

Six Vital Capitals

Insofar as the sustainability performance of organizations and other human collectives is now widely understood to consist of their impacts on vital capitals, much progress has been made over the years in terms of what they (the capitals) are and how they are defined. Indeed, capital theory in the sustainability and economics literature has more or less settled on a framework consisting of the six broad categories of capital we assess in the MultiCapital Scorecard: natural, human, social and relationship, constructed (also known as manufactured or built), economic, and intellectual.[3] To one degree or another, all six are required to ensure human well-being and that is one reason why they matter. Maintaining vital capitals in sufficient supply, therefore, is what we mean by sustainable; degrading or failing to maintain them is what we mean by unsustainable. Sustainability, then, is the study and

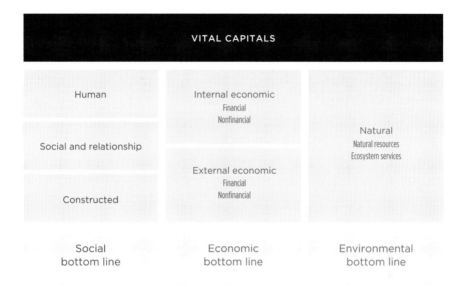

VITAL CAPITALS

Human	Internal economic	
	Financial	
	Nonfinancial	Natural
Social and relationship		Natural resources
		Ecosystem services
	External economic	
Constructed	Financial	
	Nonfinancial	

| Social | Economic | Environmental |
| bottom line | bottom line | bottom line |

Figure 2.1. Vital capitals and the triple bottom line. Here we show the capital labels we use and how they correlate to the three bottom lines.

management of human impacts on all vital capitals. Almost everything we (and especially organizations) do has impacts on natural and social capitals as well as economic consequences.

Organizational performance in general, therefore, can and should be understood in terms of what an organization's impacts on vital capitals are, relative to norms or standards for what they (the impacts) would have to be in order to be sustainable. This is the theory of performance that lies behind the MultiCapital Scorecard. To perform well is to perform sustainably, including in financial performance. If the regulative ideal for positive performance is to maintain and not degrade vital capitals, that certainly applies to financial capital as much as it does any other.

As shown in figure 2.1, the MultiCapital Scorecard focuses on five basic types of vital capital: natural, human, social and relationship, constructed, and economic (internal and external). The sixth, intellectual capital, also of course exists, but we and many others prefer to think of it as being embedded in the other five. A critical component of human capital, for example, is personal knowledge; a component of social and relationship capital is shared or mutually held knowledge; and a component of constructed capital is knowledge contained in information systems or as expressed in the material creations of the human mind. Natural capital, too, can contain intellectual capital (or knowledge) in the sense that DNA, genetic sequences, and synaptic connections in biological brains can be thought of as constituting codified information systems of one kind or another.

Figure 2.1 also shows the correlation between vital capitals and the three dimensions of the triple bottom line. It is impacts on natural capitals, for example, that determine performance in the environmental bottom line; impacts on economic capitals the economic bottom line; and so forth. This is indeed precisely how impacts on vital capitals are segregated and scored in the MultiCapital Scorecard as illustrated in chapter 3 and in part 2 of this book.

That all said, the capital definitions we rely on relative to the content of figure 2.1 are as follows:

Natural Capital

- Natural resources consist of air, land, water, minerals, flora, fauna, ecosystems, and other natural biophysical resources that humans and nonhumans alike rely on for their well-being.
- Ecosystem services consist of services or functions provided by ecosystems that humans and nonhumans alike rely on for their well-being.

Human Capital

- Human capital consists of knowledge, skills, experience, health, values, attitudes, motivation, and ethical duties and entitlements of individuals (including their intellectual capital).

Social and Relationship Capital

- Social and relationship capital consists of teams, networks, and hierarchies of individuals working together and their shared knowledge, skills, experience, health, values, attitudes, motivation, and ethical duties and entitlements (including their shared intellectual capital).

Constructed Capital

- Constructed capital refers to material objects, systems, or ecosystems created and/or cultivated by humans, including the functions they perform. It is the world of human design in which intellectual capital may also be embedded and/or expressed.

INTERNAL ECONOMIC CAPITAL

- Financial internal economic capital consists of the pool of funds available to an organization, including debt and equity finance. This description of financial capital focuses on the sources of funding, (liabilities on the balance sheet) rather than its application, which usually results in the acquisition of assets such as land, buildings, plant, and inventories or other forms of capital (for example, intellectual property rights).
- Nonfinancial internal economic capital consists of assets not recognized in internal financial capital. They may or may not also be monetized. An example is the value of brands that have been developed organically internally, but not recognized in the financial accounts.

EXTERNAL ECONOMIC CAPITAL

- Financial external economic capital consists of all financial funds available to parties outside an organization.
- Nonfinancial external economic capital consists of externally held capitals of a nonfinancial nature, which nevertheless have economic value to others. An example of natural capital in this category could be land held in California that may be impacted by the unintended adverse consequences of fracking. An example of social capital in this category might be the educational networks created by AstraZeneca and the University of Cambridge spanning translational science, basic and clinical research in life sciences, and medicine. In both these cases, an organization's impacts upon external nonfinancial capitals may have economic consequences for others, either negative or positive, which the MultiCapital Scorecard recognizes as such.

In some organizations' contexts, these individual classifications sometimes contain overlaps, or have weak borders between them. We treat these descriptions as guidelines and not strict definitions of hermetically sealed silos.

How the MultiCapital Scorecard Improves on Context-Based Sustainability

Context-Based Sustainability, the foundation of the MultiCapital Scorecard, utilizes a binary scoring system in which the impact on each vital capital is rated as either sustainable or unsustainable. It also treats each vital capital as having the same importance to the organization (and its various stakeholder groups). Its described process defines sustainability norms, standards, or thresholds that serve as performance targets for each capital impact.

These concepts have the virtue of simplicity and have been found to be adequate in practice for nonfinancial applications of Context-Based Sustainability. However, two new demands have arisen that call for consideration of the approach we call the MultiCapital Scorecard:

- The need to address financial performance and impacts on economic capitals, too, (an essential element of a complete triple bottom line approach to performance measurement and reporting) forces organizations to confront issues not previously made explicit in Context-Based Sustainability, and
- The need to use Context-Based Sustainability processes to monitor progress toward reducing unsustainability and achieving sustainability in something other than binary (yes/no) terms. Progression measurement and reporting are also needed.

Given that most if not all organizations are currently performing in unsustainable ways, a core characteristic of a useful performance measurement system would be that it be able to guide organizations toward sustainability, while recognizing and rewarding performance along the way. Since such change management efforts often span many years, progress against interim milestones, or **trajectory targets**, is an important component of performance measurement that the MultiCapital Scorecard offers.

Some implementations of Context-Based Sustainability already incorporate such trajectory targets into their internal processes (for example, trajectory targets are already featured in a multiyear context-based carbon metric developed by the Center for Sustainable Organizations).[4] An attainable interim target is an important motivational characteristic; achieving it reinforces positive action.

So while the Context-Based Sustainability performance measurement system may have its limitations (in particular for measuring progress toward sustainability), it remains valid for answering the vital question of the extent to which an organization is performing sustainably for a period in question in more absolute (binary) terms. Indeed, the sustainability norm basis of Context-Based Sustainability remains the cornerstone of the MultiCapital Scorecard.

Our challenge is therefore to focus on performance management information: how to support organizations in their endeavors to manage less unsustainably, with a view toward eventually becoming fully sustainable.

CHAPTER THREE

Putting the
MultiCapital Scorecard
into Practice

The MultiCapital Scorecard offers a sound basis for setting norms of sustainable performance. It also provides a learning framework for practitioners and thought leaders. Moreover, it has the potential to provide organizational leaders the decision support information needed to plan and advance performance toward less unsustainable futures. This means that it has to become more than a simple feedback system: It needs to "feed forward." This implies that it allows for the interpretation of performance results and offers data to support alternative courses of action. If it is to gain widespread acceptance as a mainstream planning and reporting system for organizations of all sorts, we believe management information based on the MultiCapital Scorecard should meet these criteria: It should have conceptual integrity and be meaningful, explicitly transparent, scalable, consolidated and disaggregated, actionable, reliable, and good enough (not perfect).

Conceptual Integrity

The new challenge of providing integrated reports to a wide audience of stakeholders of all sorts demands that the principles on which reports are built need to be sound and widely understood. The conceptual framework needs to withstand extreme scrutiny because it will usually be the case that some stakeholders will be disappointed with decisions and outcomes. If this were not the case, sustainable performance would not be so rare.

Since the MultiCapital Scorecard is based on a set of sound principles applied equally to all vital capitals, the reporting systems of the MultiCapital Scorecard need to be congruent, both internally and contextually. This conceptual integrity is the key characteristic that sets the MultiCapital Scorecard apart from all other corporate social responsibility or sustainability reporting processes. All others fail to ask what represents a sufficient performance of an organization in its own context.

As a result, corporate social responsibility/sustainability reports generally fail to convince users that there is a valid underlying theory of performance beyond simply doing more or less than before. In no other domain of organizational performance would such incrementalist thinking be accepted as an adequate basis for assessing performance. How can anyone believe that in a world in which humanity is breaching known planetary boundaries such marginal incrementalism is acceptable for triple bottom line reporting? It may be better than doing nothing. But serious organizational performance initiatives cry out for better.

Meaningful

Organizations across a wide spectrum of activities and in completely divergent circumstances should be able to use the MultiCapital Scorecard's reports to make sense of the sustainability of their performance. Incorporating context is a necessary, but not a sufficient, condition for meaningful interpretation of performance. Monitoring progress over time is also critical to a meaningful reporting system. Failure to capture meaningful performance condemns reporting systems to obedient compliance at best. Organizations can do much better than that and the MultiCapital Scorecard shows us how.

Whereas there are many calls from analysts for standardization of data definitions (for example, to facilitate interfirm comparisons), the resulting context-free data seldom helps leaders or investors make meaningful comparisons. Indeed, the essence of the MultiCapital Scorecard lies in the devolution of standard-setting authority to local operators in their own contexts and in their own terms, drawing on global as well as local scientific data to the maximum extent possible. This maximizes sensemaking at the operational level.

Reporting systems built on the MultiCapital Scorecard should seek to preserve meaning to stakeholders of all sorts at all levels of aggregation. Ideally, we would have a standardized and consistent methodology in use by all organizations for assessing the sustainability of their impacts on natural capitals (context-based, of course). Thresholds and allocations would always differ, but the means by which thresholds and allocations are defined would not. This is key for making meaningful comparisons between organizations. However, until such interorganizational comparisons are available, we believe that meaningful context-based metrics are preferable to technically comparable data that is context-free and therefore often meaningless. (See appendix D for guidance on how to construct and apply context-based metrics.)

Explicit Transparency

Confidence in information is greatly improved when the concepts, the data, and their sources are clearly articulated. Sharing that information with stakeholders reinforces stakeholder engagement. Reviewing, comparing, and reformulating norms, metrics, and data sources are essential to the MultiCapital Scorecard's learning processes. Transparency is therefore a cornerstone of the MultiCapital Scorecard process in which all stakeholders have access to almost all performance information. Hidden accounting contingencies, reserves, and provisions should be consigned to the past when concealment and profit-trend smoothing were the norms. Now and into the future, by contrast, all data must be made explicit and transparent to meet the needs of the open information society that is a prerequisite of a sustainable future.

Scalable

The reporting solution needs to be applicable to small operations and also capable of accommodating multinational, multiactivity organizations. Not all dimensions or characteristics need to be used by small operations or start-ups, but the investments in setting up and learning need to be capable of continuing into larger scale operations. This provides a learning pathway. (See the Sustainability Code in appendix B for a more complete description of the learning system needed.)

Consolidated and Disaggregated

Multidivisional and multinational organizations need a reporting process that allows them to consolidate the performance data to report as a single entity, while managing at lower levels of disaggregation. At both the single unit and aggregated level, the performance data needs to be meaningful.

Actionable

Management information that is meaningful also needs to be actionable. Sensemaking and interpretation processes should indicate future possible plans of action to close the gaps or to correct the course of the organization. Feed-forward loops can prompt action, but responsibilities for taking the action and ensuring its effect in practice lie with those charged with governance and leadership. Performance standards help indicate areas in need of action. Absence of standards tends to leave leaders and those charged with governance asking either "Now what?" or "So what?"

Reliable

It follows from the above that the basis for action should be reliable, within the bounds of the materiality limits applied (see chapter 7). The MultiCapital Scorecard process envisages periodic reviews to improve norm setting and correct erroneous data. Reliability will clearly improve with time and experience. In its earliest stages of implementation, it may be wise to be circumspect in taking action that may appear to be counterintuitive until independent validation is available to endorse the action.

Good Enough (Not Perfect)

From a practitioner's viewpoint, any system has to be fit for its intended purpose. Perfection is a counsel of despair, since no system can be free from criticism or error or be proven as such. Indeed, there is a paradox in the linearity of searching for perfection before implementing: Praxis feeds theory. Learning is cyclical and iterative, not linear. We can often more easily "learn from doing" (experiment in practice without a full understanding) than we can "do from learning" (implement pure theory).

The MultiCapital Scorecard is a system that helps organizations to learn by doing. Its pillars of capital theory, stakeholder engagement, sustainability, and generalizability (asking what would be the consequence if everybody behaved in the same way) are applicable from the outset, as are its performance measurement processes. But it makes no pretense at perfect knowledge. The double-loop learning process shown in figure 9.1 in chapter 9 is an explicit acknowledgement of the need to improve and refine the process as well as the assumptions that underlie the data it produces.

The performance measurement processes therefore need to meet the principle of doing the most good for the least use of resources. Organizations may strive toward perfection, but they will only allow the MultiCapital Scorecard to develop its full potential once many users are able to pool their collective wisdom from using its performance measurement processes in practice.

Scoring and Weighting in the MultiCapital Scorecard

The MultiCapital Scorecard offers organizations ways of performing in explicit terms that many attempt to do implicitly, namely, measuring, managing, and reporting the importance of their various vital capital impacts. Furthermore, the work that goes into MultiCapital Scorecard performance metrics recognizes progression toward or away from sustainability goals.

To meet the needs for a more nuanced approach to performance measurement and to allow organizations to attach varying degrees of importance to the impacts they have, or don't have, on vital capitals, we put forward a scoring and weighting scheme, which comprises the following integrated elements:

- Sustainability norms, the benchmarks for sustainable performance
- Trajectory targets, comprising multiperiod milestones for progression toward achievement of sustainability norms
- A progression performance scoring schema, reflecting different levels of performance in each year
- Weighting of capital impacts, reflecting the organization's view of the importance of each
- Sizing of operations, to allow meaningful consolidation of units of differing dimensions

Each of the elements is explained further below.

Sustainability Norms (Benchmarks for Sustainable Performance)

Of central importance in the MultiCapital Scorecard is the idea that vital capitals are finite in supply and that human activities can either increase or decrease their amounts. Managing organizational performance, therefore, can usefully be thought of as managing impacts on vital capitals, or as capital impact management. Indeed, organizations can be said to be duty-bound to manage their impacts on vital capitals insofar as their impacts can affect the well-being of others.

Some such duties may be legally based (for example, toward shareholders, employees, customers, trading partners, and so on). Other duties, such as toward neighbors or local community members, are independent of any contracts or business arrangements that may exist between them. They arise from concepts of natural justice. Rawls gives the example of the duty to others in distress to do one's best to assist without jeopardizing one's own future.[1] This is the moral and ethical foundation of stakeholder theory on which the MultiCapital Scorecard is based.

All of this, in turn, gives rise to performance criteria we refer to as sustainability norms—those standards of performance that are tied to an understanding of what stakeholders require in the way of vital capitals in order to maintain their well-being (see figure 3.1). In general, organizational performance should put neither the sufficiency of such capitals nor the well-being of those who rely on them (stakeholders) at risk.

To specify sustainability norms in detail, we make an all-important distinction between thresholds and allocations. A threshold is either an upper or lower limit in the supply of a capital stock. These are limits that either must not be crossed, such as water consumption in a watershed, or must be maintained at some level, such as government services in a municipality. The first is a case of constraining resource use in order to not deplete it; the second is a case of continually producing resources so that the carrying capacity does not diminish. Here we can say that all but the natural capitals are anthropogenic, and so sustainability norms in the case of natural capitals tend to be expressed in terms of constrained use or consumption. Norms

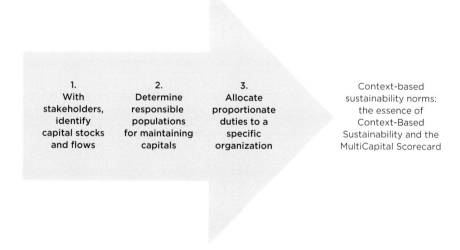

Figure 3.1. The logic of defining sustainability norms. This three-stage process generates the sustainability norms that answer the question of "How much is enough to be sustainable?"
Adapted from *Corporate Sustainability Management* by Mark W. McElroy and Jo M. L. van Engelen, Routledge 2012.

for the other capitals, by contrast, tend to be expressed in terms of ongoing levels of production. Anthropogenic capitals are just that: human-made. Natural capitals are not.

Once thresholds for vital capitals have been determined, allocations must be made according to which fair, just, and proportionate shares of either the resources involved (natural capital) or the burden to continually produce and maintain them (all of the other capitals) are assigned to individual organizations (or facilities in the case of strictly local impacts). Again, let's take water use as an example. Water is a finite resource and is also geographically distributed. Renewable levels of water supplies can be thought of as varying by location (that is, by watershed). The total volume of available renewable water in a watershed would be the contextually relevant threshold when attempting to define a sustainability norm for water use. But that still wouldn't tell us what an individual organization's fair share of water should be in the watershed. That would call for an allocation.

In the case of entitlements to use water, allocations can be made by reference to an organization's size. This can be done, for example, by correlating a share of available renewable water to an organization's proportionate contribution to gross domestic product (GDP) in the same region or to the size of its workforce relative to the human population in the same geography. These approaches to making fair, just, and proportionate allocations apply in cases where there are multiple parties involved who are either sharing access to a limited natural resource or who are co-responsible for continually producing anthropogenic resources (for example, upholding fair trade conditions in a supply chain).

Some capital maintenance responsibilities are, by contrast, solely held by an organization and are not shared with others at all. This might include the responsibility to pay a livable wage; or maintain the safety of working conditions; or ensure that products are safe. These are all sustainability norms for which organizations tend to be solely responsible. Other examples, such as the water case, involve sustainability norms where organizations are only co-responsible for the resources involved. Accountability for maintaining (or living within the carrying capacity of) the natural resources involved is shared, in which case organizations can only be held accountable for their fair, just, and proportionate share of the joint responsibility.

Putting the MultiCapital Scorecard into Practice

As we learned in chapter 1 and illustrated in figure 3.1, organizations are responsible for defining their own sustainability norms. In some cases, however, formal if not legislated guidance will be available as input to making such decisions. This is especially the case with respect to environmental impacts on natural capital. Science-based guidance for identifying contextually relevant thresholds for water use and greenhouse gas emissions is now widely available and has been incorporated into the practice of Context-Based Sustainability for years.[2] The same is true for certain other areas of impact, such as locally relevant livable wage standards.

That said, it is still most often the case that formal guidance or standards for setting sustainability norms, whatever that might mean, are not themselves the norm yet. Indeed, everything other than financial reporting by publicly traded firms is still purely voluntary. The optimists in us would like to believe that this will not always be the case. And so with that in mind, it is perhaps best to think of our present circumstance as one in which context-based, triple bottom line management is still very much in its formative stage. Best practices are still being developed. Trial and error rules the day.

Still, as we say more than once in this book, "better to be approximately right than precisely wrong." It is precisely wrong, that is, to refrain from measuring, managing, and reporting performance in terms of context-based impacts on vital capitals simply because consensus-based standards for doing so do not yet exist. Better to be measuring performance against debatable sustainability norms than no sustainability norms at all. Here is how Donella Meadows put it way back in 1998:[3]

> It is tempting, given all the caveats and challenges . . . in every report on sustainable development indicators, to be daunted, to postpone the task, to wait for more thinking, more modeling, more agreement—to wait for perfection. While we are waiting for perfection, fisheries are collapsing, greenhouse gases are accumulating, species are disappearing, soils are eroding, forests are overcut, people are suffering. So it is important to get some preliminary indicators out there and into use, the best we can do at the moment. That way, as long as we are willing to evaluate and make corrections, we can start to learn, which is the only way we can ever achieve sustainable development.

So rather than wait for perfection, it is perfection that should wait for us: for the benefits of our learning to inform effective action. While it might be comforting to have consensus-based sustainability norms across the board, it certainly isn't required in order to take effective action. In truth, consensus is a luxury we cannot afford to wait for. Better to just plunge ahead and learn as we go. (See appendix D for more guidance on how to define sustainability norms and specify context-based metrics.)

Trajectory Targets (Comprising Multiperiod Milestones for Progression toward Sustainability Norms)

The MultiCapital Scorecard offers learning processes for organizations to address long-term change programs. We offer no quick fixes, but encourage organizations of all sorts to work progressively toward thinking and behaving in new ways. These organizational learning journeys may take many years. The double-loop review process in the MultiCapital Scorecard explicitly con-templates a long-time scale with periodic reviews.

Consequently, the ideal multiple capital performance accounting system would monitor progress against interim "milestones" along the road of the learning journey. For example, consider a case of living wages. If the sustain-ability norm for the lowest paid worker's living wage in 2016 were $35,000, but 2015 performance is at $26,000, then $35,000 (adjusted for inflation to $38,000) may be set as the norm to be achieved in four years' time. On that trajectory, interim targets of $29,000, $32,000, and $35,000 may be set for years one, two, and three, respectively, of a change program.

In order to set trajectories that are stretching, but achievable, it is import-ant to anchor the trajectory times and targets in scientifically determined scenarios that accomplish sustainability norms with satisfactory outcomes, wherever these are available. Other contextual information, including an organization's or its stakeholders' own data, should be called on in the absence of scientific trajectory data. For market-based performances (for example, returns on equity capital), peer group market performances may be drawn on to support the definition of trajectory targets, but always in relation to sustainability norms.

The incorporation of trajectory targets as an integral element of the performance measurement information system brings to the executives' meeting room table a monitor of progress. The monitor can work at aggregate annual levels, but can also be broken down to subprojects with updates on monthly reporting timetables. This degree of granularity reduces the global targets and distant aims to everyday tasks with variances and corrective actions needed as a matter of urgency. In the fight for space on the monthly governance agenda, the projects that can most easily plot progress against accepted norms are easiest to understand and accept. Trajectory targets are therefore critical to making multiple capital performance accounting a vital part of the life of the organization.

Progression Performance Scoring Schema (Reflecting Different Levels of Performance in Each Year)

To assess performance relative to trajectory targets and sustainability norms, the MultiCapital Scorecard uses the point-based scoring system shown in table 3.1.

TABLE 3.1. The Progression Performance Scoring Schema for the MultiCapital Scorecard

NUMERIC SCORE	SCORE DEFINITION
+3	Meeting or exceeding the sustainability norm for the year
+2	Meeting or exceeding the year's trajectory target, but falling short of the sustainability norm
+1	Improving upon the previous year's performance, but not meeting the year's trajectory target, or any year of improving performance, while having no such targets at all (sustainability norms or trajectory targets)
0	Maintaining the previous year's performance, while not meeting the year's trajectory target
-1	A 1-year regression in performance, while not meeting the year's trajectory target
-2	A 2-year regression in performance, while not meeting the year's trajectory target
-3	A 3-or-more year regression in performance, while not meeting the year's trajectory target, or any year of worsening performance while having no such targets at all (sustainability norm or trajectory target)

Scores of +1, +2, and +3 differentiate into broad categories the degree of progress made in each area for each year. Only the +3 score represents fully sustainable performance, but +1 and +2 scores acknowledge degrees of progression toward achieving sustainability. However, these are all positive scores and not everywhere is progression positive.

A complete scoring system, therefore, should address negative performance, too. It seems right for a fair system to penalize the destruction of (or failure to create or maintain) vital capitals proportionately to the same degree to which it recognizes positive impacts on them.

However, the fact is that any performance that fails to meet sustainability norms is actively or passively eroding vital capitals in the interim trajectory period. We therefore propose negative scores for negative progression.

We reserve the maximum negative score (-3) for cases where performance is either persistently worsening the unsustainable impacts or where there is an absence of any meaningful standard setting. Since most organizations currently fail to ask "how much is enough to be sustainable?", this score is often to be expected in organizations starting out on the MultiCapital Scorecard process. It follows that a substantial improvement is achievable by simply getting started. This may create "distortions" in progression reporting if viewed through the lens of technical performance. However, in many organizations it is the very act of *not* getting started that holds them back from the journey of self-discovery. Our behavioral approach therefore unapologetically offers a big bonus to organizations that do make a start in asking how much is enough to be sustainable.

The minimum negative score (-1) will occur in reality in many cases where a year's performance slips below a prior year's level and below trajectory targets. It signifies, therefore, a setback, but is not usually an indicator of willful capital destruction. However, a two-year regression (-2) signifies a greater cause for concern and is scored accordingly.

The balance we have had to strike here is between simplicity in interpretation by users and strict linearity in measuring progression in a more sophisticated but less intelligible way. We consider the outcome to deliver a reasonable balance in favor of users who ultimately need to take corrective action on the ground. But if organizations in their own contexts find preferable means of scoring performance in an even-handed manner, that is all to the good. Be wary of any system that only awards positive scores.

If a better system is accomplished, dear reader, please let us, the authors, know your process so that we may be able to share the learning in future editions of the MultiCapital Scorecard.

Weighting of Capital Impacts (Reflecting the Organization's View of the Importance of Each)

A critical task of management and those charged with governance of all organizations is to balance the competing demands of stakeholders to the duties they believe they are owed. Attaching weights to the importance the organization places on the duties to have specified impacts on each vital capital enables such importance to be discussed explicitly and to be easily communicated to all stakeholders. Weighting is not an essential component of the MultiCapital Scorecard, but we believe it offers significant advantages to facilitating stakeholder dialogue. It also ensures that the results of the dialogue are translated into the performance accounting process and will likely be important to interpreting the MultiCapital Scorecard in many if not most organizations. Still, we do not seek to prescribe the range of weights accorded to the various areas of impact.

In part 2 of this book, we provide worked examples for a hypothetical corporation. There, for illustrative purposes only, we adopt a scale of weights in which 1 represents the least important duty and 5 the most important. Suffice it to say that the judgment needed to determine the relative importance of the weights to be adopted is essentially context-specific. Each organization needs its own procedures, guidelines, and decision mechanisms. But they will all result in much more meaningful outputs of the MultiCapital Scorecard process than any weightings that may be set in a context-free manner.

To avoid gaming the system or distorting the sizing of units within a consolidating group, a standard budget of weighting points per unit might be centrally defined with all weighting points to then be used. Alternatively, an organization may choose not to weight at all.

Sizing of Operations (to Allow for Meaningful Consolidation of Units of Differing Dimensions)

Financial consolidations (aggregations that are usually done in denominations of the reporting currency of the holding entity) reflect the size of their subsidiaries' impacts on financial capital in absolute terms: financial bottom line profit. This in itself imposes a means of incorporating size differentials. If small subsidiaries generate large profits, then they are given the correspondingly large weight of their impact on the group's financial capital.

In MultiCapital Scorecard terms, there is no such absolute metric as money. The performance of each unit is reported as the extent to which it achieves its sustainability norms (or trajectory targets). Without any sizing adjustments, the impacts of extremely small and extremely large units or subdivisions could unjustifiably cancel each other out. Size does matter in consolidations.

Apart from the imbalance that forgoing sizing adjustments implies, it also opens the door to gaming the system. If all highly unsustainable units are grouped into a single very large reporting entity, while all the nearly sustainable units are reported separately as very small but well-performing reporting units, the consolidated total would be entirely unrepresentative of the underlying reality. This flaw could completely undermine the meaning of the consolidated totals in practice.

We propose that the reporting entity should select a representative index or multiple indices for sizing its component parts. For the purposes of consolidations, we shall refer to such parts as units. In a business, the index might be the turnover or sales value of the units. In a healthcare system, it might be the number of patients that are dealt with. In a university, it may be the number of students. There are many other indicators of size that may be appropriate to different organizations. Each consolidation entity should choose one that it (or its sector) recognizes as most meaningful. The proportion that each unit represents in the consolidated reporting entity can then be established as a percentage. Applying that percentage to the performance scores of each unit (weighted or unweighted, depending on the choice of the organization) will allow a meaningful consolidation of the scores of all units together. The worked examples in part 2 of this book adopt sales value as the sizing index for consolidation purposes.

It is, of course, open to each organization to set its own sizing criteria. These may differ for the different parts of the triple bottom line. For example, a group may choose to size their economic impacts by the value of their cash flows or capital employed, while sizing their environmental impacts by their tonnage of greenhouse gas emissions. As in all cases, the balance has to be drawn between the potential relevance of more refined methodologies and the effort required to produce more nuanced consolidation protocols.

Adopting these scoring and weighting mechanisms, the MultiCapital Scorecard extends the principles of Context-Based Sustainability measurement (which give binary results) to provide the managers and directors of organizations with an indication of their progression toward eliminating unsustainable performance. The undoubted imperfections in the process will be improved on in practice as each organization adds to its collective learning and continuous improvement in its own unique context. The Sustainability Code in appendix B sets out eleven principles to guide the learning experience.

The MultiCapital Scorecard as a Stepwise Methodology

We now turn our attention to the general flow of MultiCapital Scorecard projects. In practice, MultiCapital Scorecard projects follow a three-step process:

1. Scoping and materiality
2. Areas of impact development
3. Scorecard implementation

Step One: Scoping and Materiality

In this step, the boundaries of an organization or entity to be assessed using the MultiCapital Scorecard are defined, as are the relevant and material **areas of impact** (**AOIs**) to be considered. (See also chapter 7 for more on materiality.) AOIs, as constructs, are the fundamental units of interest in the MultiCapital Scorecard toward which all of our attention is directed. In the MultiCapital Scorecard, AOIs are defined as the discrete impacts of organizations on vital capitals. The referents of interest to us, that is, are impacts on capitals.

That said, we are only interested in those impacts for which corresponding duties or obligations to stakeholders exist.[4] An organization's impacts on water resources, for example, are nearly always of interest because of their importance to others. In other words, the fact that a resource an organization is using is being shared with others gives rise to a duty or obligation to manage its impacts accordingly (with their interests in mind so as to at least not do harm to them or the resources they rely on). The same holds true for other natural capitals.

Not all impacts on capitals of importance to the well-being of others are necessarily material in the eyes of the MultiCapital Scorecard.[5] Materiality only applies to impacts on capitals that are of importance to stakeholders. Third parties, such as dependents of employees or other stakeholders, do not apply. (Again, see chapter 7 for more on materiality.) Remember, in the MultiCapital Scorecard, a stakeholder is anyone to whom the organization owes a duty or obligation to manage its impacts on vital capitals in ways that can affect their well-being. In some cases, such a responsibility can arise by virtue of the impacts an organization is already having (such as when a company's activities affect local air quality). In other cases, stakeholders receive their standing as a consequence of contracts or agreements they have entered into—be they employment agreements, purchase agreements, or otherwise—or as bestowed on them by morality or law. In all cases, material AOIs are organization-specific and are determined by their managers and directors themselves, with the input and involvement of others as they see fit.[6]

Materiality determinations in the MultiCapital Scorecard therefore (a) only apply to AOIs and (b) can only result in the designation of AOIs as material in cases where the interests of bona fide stakeholders are involved to whom corresponding duties or obligations are owed by an organization to manage its impacts on capitals in some way. Most organizations, for example, have a fiduciary duty to manage their impacts on financial capital for the benefit of their shareholders. Obeying the law and fulfilling the terms of agreements with employees, customers, and suppliers are some others.

Step Two: Areas of Impact Development

Once a material set or portfolio of AOIs has been identified for an organization, each of the associated AOIs must be further researched and developed in preparation for the role it will play in measurement and reporting. This process has two parts to it. First is the specification of sustainability norms or goals, and second is the development of an associated data collection protocol.

As explained previously, we define sustainability norms as standards of performance for what an organization's impacts on vital capitals must be in order to be sufficient, sustainable, and supportive of stakeholder well-being. And sometimes the sustainability norms identified by an organization for particular AOIs will not be achievable anytime soon, in which case the MultiCapital Scorecard allows for the specification of trajectory targets as interim goals.

Once sustainability norms and trajectory targets have been defined for individual AOIs, data collection protocols for each must be developed. A data collection protocol is a system for gathering the data required to describe an organization's impacts, and such data can then be used to populate a MultiCapital Scorecard. In general, a protocol will have people, process, and technology dimensions. The people dimension will identify the parties responsible for gathering the data; the process dimension will determine when and how the data should be collected; and the technology dimension will specify the role of technology, if any, in capturing, computing, and reporting the data required.

Once the sustainability norms and trajectory targets and data collection protocols for each AOI have been defined, the results are recorded for each AOI, as shown in table 3.2. That table shows greenhouse gas (GHG) emissions over a five-year period, for which the corresponding AOI of interest is the climate system.

In table 3.2 the sustainability norm for greenhouse gas emissions is "0" emissions in all years. In order to get to that level, though, a steady progression of decreases in emissions is required over time, as specified in science-based models over multiple decades if not longer. The example included here simply shows the application of such a model to the first five years of a strategy

TABLE 3.2. Performance Goals and Scores for a Climate System AOI

	2015	2016	2017	2018	2019
Sustainability Norm	0	0	0	0	0
Trajectory Targets	24,000	23,333	21,667	20,000	18,333
GHG Emissions (metric tons)	25,000	24,100	21,650	20,000	18,300
Progression Score	0	1	2	2	2

starting with a baseline year of 2015. Incremental decreases in allowable emissions are then identified as trajectory targets for the four years that follow. The "GHG Emissions (metric tons)" row then reports actual emissions for a five-year period as of the end of 2019.

The lowermost "Progression Score" row then comes into play as an illustration of how we score performance against sustainability norms and trajectory targets in the MultiCapital Scorecard. We refer to these scores as *progression scores* because they tell us how an organization's actual impacts on vital capitals compare to the sustainability norms and trajectory targets we have defined for each AOI. The indicators we use to do so comprise the seven-point scale or schema shown in table 3.1.

As the example in table 3.2 shows, the hypothetical case we present here features scores of no better than "2" in any given year, since at no time were actual greenhouse gas emissions "0" metric tons or less. Short of that, the best an organization can do is score a "2," which is defined as "meeting or exceeding the year's trajectory target, but falling short of the sustainability norm."

Step Three: Scorecard Implementation

Once sustainability norms, trajectory targets, data collection protocols, and progression scores have been obtained for each AOI, it is time to integrate and report them in a MultiCapital Scorecard of the sort shown in figure 3.2. For demonstration purposes, figure 3.2 shows a fully configured scorecard for the fictitious organization we've created to demonstrate the MultiCapital Scorecard in this book, Company ABC. The scorecard shown is for 2019 and illustrates a case in which Company ABC has identified nine AOIs for which duties and obligations to manage its impacts on vital capitals exist. The nine

2019 MultiCapital Scorecard for Company ABC

Vital capitals*

- ■ Natural
- ■ Constructed
- ■ Human
- ■ Social and Relationship
- ■ Internal Economic—Financial
- ■ Internal Economic—Nonfinancial
- ■ External Economic—Financial
- ■ External Economic—Nonfinancial

BOTTOM LINES	AREAS OF IMPACT	CAPITAL IMPACTS	A Progression score	B Weight	C Weighted score (AxB)	Fully sustainable score (Bx3)	D Gap to fully sustainable (D-C)	Area of impact (AOI) bottom line (C/D)	TRIPLE BOTTOM LINE SCORES
Social	Living wage	■	3	1	3	3	0	100%	
	Workplace safety	■ ■ ■	3	5	15	15	0	100%	83%
	Innovative capacity	■ ■ ■	1	2	2	6	4	33%	
Economic	Equity	■	3	5	15	15	0	100%	
	Debt	■	2	1	2	3	1	67%	90%
	Competitive practices	■	2	1	2	3	1	67%	
Environmental	Water supplies	■	3	3	9	9	0	100%	
	Solid waste	■	2	2	4	6	2	67%	77%
	The climate system	■	2	5	10	15	5	67%	
	OVERALL PERFORMANCE				62	75	13		83%

Note: Areas of Impact shown here are purely illustrative and are always organization-specific.
* Intellectual Capital is typically embedded in most of the others.

Figure 3.2. An annual MultiCapital Scorecard. This fully configured scorecard illustrates how hypothetical Company ABC reported its impacts on vital capitals for 2019.

AOIs, in turn, have been arranged in terms of the three bottom lines they correspond to (refer to figure 2.1 to see the basis for making these associations).[7]

We'll walk readers through worked examples of the scorecard in detail in part 2; but for now, looking at the "The climate system" row at the bottom of the scorecard can elucidate the scorecard's calculations. It assumes the same climate system sustainability norms and trajectory targets that were shown in table 3.2. Starting with the progression score (column A), Company ABC more than met its trajectory target in 2019 by reducing its emissions to a level that fell below allowable limits, while still failing to achieve the sustainability norm of "0" emissions. It thereby earned a score of "2" for that year as defined in the progression performance schema shown in table 3.1.

Next we see that a weight (column B) of 5 has been assigned to the climate system AOI, which was taken from the importance attached to it by management on a scale of 1 to 5, according to which 1 is a low priority and 5 is a high priority. This is a decision that would have been made during the construction of Company ABC's scorecard, if not beforehand as the overall mix of its AOIs was coming into view.

Next we compute the weighted score (column C) for each AOI, which for the climate system was 10 (progression score of 2, multiplied by a weight of 5). After that, we compute the maximum possible fully sustainable score (column D) for each AOI, which for the climate system is 15 (best possible progression score of 3, multiplied by a weight of 5); and we then compare the weighted score with the fully sustainable score to determine the size of the gap between them, if any. In the case of the climate system, there is a gap of 5 points. In terms of its actual performance relative to the sustainability norms for impacts on the climate system, then, Company ABC earned a score of 67 percent (10 out of 15 possible points).

Beyond providing scores for each AOI, the MultiCapital Scorecard also calculates performance scores by bottom line and for organizations as a whole. For bottom line calculations, we simply total up all weighted and fully sustainable scores in each case, separately, and then express them as the quotient of the one over the other (weighted score total/fully sustainable score total). That gives us quantitative performance scores for each bottom line. We then do the same thing for the entire portfolio, and out of that comes an overall triple bottom line score for the organization as a whole (83 percent in the case of the example shown in figure 3.2). We know of no other performance accounting system that does this, and yet it needs to be done in order for meaningful, integrated triple bottom line assessments to occur.

CHAPTER FOUR

Financial Capitals in the MultiCapital Scorecard

A key premise of the MultiCapital Scorecard is that all of the principles that underpin Context-Based Sustainability apply equally to all capitals, including financial and other economic capital. Context-Based Sustainability, for example, requires that we identify stakeholders, relevant vital capitals, and their associated stocks and flows. In the case of financial capitals, there are two broad categories of capital to consider: equity capital (otherwise known as shareholders' funds) and debt; the stakeholders involved are shareholders and lenders, respectively.

We deal with these categories individually in the pages to come, but there is one matter that deserves special attention. It is the question of leverage, gearing, or indebtedness: that is to say, the proportion of funding that is provided by lenders as compared to the proportion provided by equity investors. This is referred to as the **capital structure**.

In 1958, Franco Modigliani and Merton Miller published their theory that under certain conditions, the relative amounts of debt and equity in a business should have no bearing on the value of the firm.[1] Neither should the flows of dividends they pay. This theory is known as the capital structure irrelevance theory and it applies to financial capitals only.

However, the "certain conditions" they specified (such as perfect information, no taxes, equal borrowing costs for all, and perfect markets) are never to be found together in practice. Therefore, most financial practitioners agree that capital structure is important to investors and by implication to all other stakeholders, too. (Indeed, many observers attribute the causes of the financial crisis of Western economies in 2008 to excessive levels of institutional, corporate, and personal borrowing. Markets alone were proven incapable of resolving the crisis. Political leaders decided to borrow from future generations to avoid economic collapse and its social fallout.)

Conventional financial wisdom says that as borrowing costs are usually lower than the costs of equity capital (and are also tax deductible), a judicious use of debt financing reduces the total cost of capital. But excessive levels of debt increase the financial risk borne by the business, as they impose interest charges that act as fixed costs, "leveraging" residual profits to fluctuate more extremely than would be the case in a fully equity-financed business. Organizations that fail to meet their interest charges expose themselves and all their stakeholders to liquidation, insolvency, or other extreme measures imposed by lenders to salvage their loans.

Equity investors that rightly considered themselves the owners when times were good lose all control (and their equity value) when times are bad. Once the viability of an organization is jeopardized, it loses its ability to honor any of the duties and obligations (legal, moral, and ethical) that it had assumed. Stakeholders of all sorts then discover that they hold a stake in nothing at all.

We the authors recognize that the matter of capital structure, as in so many other domains of organizational life, needs to be considered in a holistic manner in the context of the organization. Capital structure, therefore, should find a place on the agenda of the main governance body of all organizations. Alongside purpose, values, and mission, capital structure should feed into the strategic discussions and plans of organizations of all sorts.

Moreover, in a world in which multiple capitals are recognized, the MultiCapital Scorecard can provide a framework within which the relationships between all vital capitals can be considered in relation to one another in the specific context of the organization. The organization's duties of balance and optimization extend, therefore, beyond the strict confines of each individual area of impact or vital capital. There is no simple algorithm that allows an organization to optimize its mix of capitals or impacts on capitals. This is where the art of management meets the science of measurement. Neither alone is good enough, but sensitive management armed with the best measurement available is the best we can offer in the current state of affairs.

We now consider the main components of financial capital: equity and debt.

Equity

For corporate equity capital, the relevant stakeholders are the shareholders. They may have many expectations of the organization, including growing social capital and reducing its environmental footprint. The MultiCapital Scorecard will help them follow performance in these areas better than any other system we know. However, many will consider that the financial component of their invested capital will be best protected by ensuring a constant stream of earnings flows from the operations of the organization. Traditionally thought of as profits, these excesses of income over costs allow dividends to be paid to equity investors or provide funds to be reinvested in the organization. In either case, the flows associated with the equity investment are the earnings net of all costs (including the cost of the capital employed in the organization). Maintaining a flow of such earnings into the organization at a level that meets the needs of investors ensures that financial performance to service the equity capital is sustainable.

For organizations other than companies or for-profit businesses, the equity capital equivalent may be provided by trustees, donors, governments, or other individuals, or by entities that do not demand an interest charge on their capital contributions. But the same principles apply to them as to other stakeholders. Their minimum requirements need to be identified to feed into the financial (and other) sustainability norms.

It is clear that the expressed needs of all investors in terms of returns required on their invested capital have to be validated, just as all other stakeholders' expressed needs have to be validated by reference to similar group expectations. In the case of equity investors, this can usually be done by reference to the market returns earned by investors in similar risk categories.

We believe that the level of returns appropriate to the MultiCapital Scorecard concept is the opportunity cost of capital; that is to say, the return below which equity investors would choose to withdraw their funding. It is conceptually close to the cut-off rate of return that investors use in their investment appraisal calculations. If investors would turn down an investment returning 5 percent per year, but would accept an investment returning 7 percent per year, we might conclude (all other things being equal) that their opportunity cost of capital for that investment is between 5 percent and 7 percent.

The earnings stream after charging a cost for the capital it employs is called **residual income**. Conventional accounts make no specific charge for the use of equity capital because equity investors own all the profit or loss generated by the business. But it is an error to assume that there is no cost of using equity capital. Because the MultiCapital Scorecard asks how much is enough to be sustainable, an estimate needs to be made of the appropriate cost of equity in order to derive the residual income. In short, this is the periodic income stream generated by the organization after deducting the opportunity cost of the capital invested in it. It measures the impact that the organization has on the financial capital it uses after allowing for all its cost. This concept is sometimes called economic profit. Earnings streams of residual income that are negative are not sustainable. Zero or positive residual income is sustainable as it covers the financial costs, duties, and obligations owed to equity investors. For the sake of clarity, we should point out that there is no legal duty to earn a particular return for investors. But as in other areas of application of the MultiCapital Scorecard, we are asking stakeholders what they consider to be the moral, ethical, or other duties the organization owes them. In this case, it is an economic duty, not a legally quantified one.

This underlines the validity of the concept of the MultiCapital Scorecard as it replicates for the financial stakeholder exactly the principles that it applies to all other stakeholders.

The principle of residual income has been widely accepted since 1890 when Alfred Marshall published his *Principles of Economics*.[2] Edgar Edwards and Philip Bell endorsed it in 1961, as did David Solomons in 1965.[3] The late Clive Emmanuel and David Otley revalidated the concept in 1976, in the *Journal of Business Finance & Accounting*.[4] Peter Drucker expressed the idea succinctly in 1995: "Until a business returns a profit that is greater than its cost of capital, it does not create [*economic*] wealth; it destroys it."[5] A further endorsement comes from Stern Stewart & Co., which adopted the residual income principle for its widely implemented, branded process that determines how much value an organization creates in economic terms (that is, economic value added).[6]

Expressing financial value in "real terms" means correcting for the inflationary distortion of the elastic measuring rod used for measuring financial performance, namely money. This, too, has been widely accepted for many decades as a valid principle, particularly so in countries that have suffered high inflation. Several accounting adjustments (see appendix E) are required to be applied to traditional historic cost accounts; but for the lay person, the fact that the dollar, euro, or pound of today is not worth what is was worth ten years ago seems obvious. That is the reason why inflation-corrected income figures are required to understand the real impact over time on financial capital. (Appendix E shows other adjustments that may be required as well.)

Real terms residual income therefore has a long heritage of being based on accepted principles. There are many disputes about their practical implementation, but few about their validity in principle.

For its part, the MultiCapital Scorecard asks all other nonfinancial-related stakeholders to articulate their expectations from the organization in question. Real terms residual income does exactly that for shareholders. Zero real terms residual income is therefore eminently well-suited to establishing the minimum financial threshold norms that shareholders can reasonably expect from their investments.

Debt

Lenders require interest payments on their loans. Financial accounts (that are legally required almost everywhere) take account of interest payments, since they are legal obligations.

In nominal terms, establishing the stakeholder expectations of lenders is fairly straightforward. Debt servicing costs and cash flows are routinely taken into account in financial accounts.

TABLE 4.1. The Real Cost of Debt

	VALUES	% OF NOMINAL VALUE OF LOAN
Nominal value of loan at start of the year	€1,000,000	100%
Interest paid at 8% nominal rate	€(80,000)	(8.0)%
Taxation relief at 30% on interest paid	€4,000	2.4%
After-tax cost of interest paid	€(56,000)	(5.6)%
Real value of loan at end of the year	€970,000	97%
Holding gain on loan for one year	€30,000	3.0%
Real after-tax interest net of holding gain	€(26,000)	(2.6)%

However, real terms accounting requires adjustments to both the capital values of debt and to the after-tax annual cost of servicing the debt. Inflation has the effect of reducing the real terms cost of repaying the outstanding loan capital. A million euro (€) loan repayable after a year in an economy in which inflation is running at 3 percent per year will be repaid at 97 percent of its original value in real terms. Meanwhile, its interest cost, say 8 percent per year, will have been tax deductible, let us assume by a 30 percent income tax rate. Nominal after-tax interest cost has therefore been 5.6 percent (70 percent of 8 percent) in the year, from which the 3 percent reduction in the real value of the loan should be deducted. The resulting after-tax real terms cost of the debt is therefore 2.6 percent in this simple example. See table 4.1 for a layout of the calculation made here: It illustrates the real terms cost of debt taken into account in the weighted cost of capital calculation.

Practice of the MultiCapital Scorecard with Respect to Financial Performance

As in the case of the environmental and social bottom lines, incorporating financial performance in the MultiCapital Scorecard starts with identification of the relevant stakeholders. In commercial organizations, it is usually clear who the financial stakeholders are. They are generally equity holders (shareholders, owners, and partners) or lenders (banks, bond holders, and creditors). It is important to distinguish between these two groups; financial accounting treats them very differently.

Equity holders receive dividend payments from any profits made from operations, but are not owed any particular level of financial return. Moreover, their invested capital is at risk, since they rank last for repayment in cases of winding up.

Lenders usually have legally binding contracts with the organization for the repayment of the monies lent and for the payment of interest on the outstanding balances owed. When winding up an organization for bankruptcy or insolvency, any money available for distribution usually goes first to lenders and the tax authorities. Only if funds remain after paying legal liabilities do equity investors receive any repayment of funds they have invested.

However, traditional accounts never specify the expectations of equity investors. As owners of the organization, equity holders are legally entitled to the whole of the income stream (profits or losses) after all legal liabilities have been taken into account.

Real terms residual income in the MultiCapital Scorecard seeks to establish for the equity investors a sustainability norm that meets their opportunity cost of capital. That is to say, it answers the question, "How much income do the financial stakeholders need in order to maintain their investment in the organization?" or "How much do they need before they withdraw their investments?" This question puts all stakeholders on the same level playing field in terms of principles. A sustainable organization needs to meet all these obligations. If it fails to meet them all, it is not sustainable in principle; or perhaps it is sustainable in some areas, but not in others.

The wish lists of all stakeholders need to be validated against peer group and other external reference points. And so it is for financial stakeholders, too. In the case of financial returns to financial investors in quoted companies, there is a wealth of data available that offers market-based evidence of comparable organizations. The opportunity costs of equity capital provided by the stakeholder engagement process can thereby be validated. In other organizations, peer group returns on equity may be used.

In many organizations, the individual financial capital sources of equity and debt cannot be easily separated. In particular, subsidiaries of holding companies that raise their finances centrally may receive (and give) their funds on a blended funding basis. Projects for which central approval is needed will be funded from the center. It will not be clear where the funds came from; they may be a mixture of debt and equity. Similarly, the remittances from the subsidiaries to the holding company will often not distinguish which sources of funding they are servicing.

In such cases, it may be appropriate to compute an average cost of capital to be applied to all new project financing. It is coherent to use such a weighted average cost of capital to determine the residual income.

The real terms cost of the capital employed by the organization can be expressed as a weighted average of the costs of equity and of debt as illustrated in table 4.2.

In the example we provide, the real terms income for a year would be charged with a cost of capital of €226,000 for the use of €3,000,000 total capital employed in the organization for the year. Let us therefore assume for this simplified example that the volumes of capital employed are exactly in line with the expected norms and the cost per annum were exactly in line with the sustainability norms, too. Then, if the resulting real terms income generated in the period is positive or zero, the financial performance may be considered sustainable. If it is negative, the financial performance for the period is unsustainable—it fails to meet the threshold for sustainable performance. Of course reality seldom pans out so conveniently in line with targets, and so there are many other possible outcomes, but the example serves to demonstrate the principle.

It is worth emphasizing that this real terms residual income measurement concept can be of great value to all organizations, whether or not they adopt it in pursuit of their multiple capital objectives. It is a concept that lends itself to both high-level strategic analysis and operational-level short-term performance measurement. However, in practice, care needs to be taken to

TABLE 4.2. The Weighted Average Cost of Capital

REAL TERMS	VOLUME	COST % PER YEAR	COST € PER YEAR
Equity	€2,000,000	10.00%	€200,000
Debt	€1,000,000	2.60%	€26,000
Total Capital	€3,000,000	7.53%	€226,000

The Importance of
Speedy Administrative Work

One organization implemented a real terms residual income process with so many adjustments and refinements to its reported profits that they took many months to prepare. As a consequence, at every board meeting directors were presented with financial accounts, but without real terms residual income numbers (ever). This of course indicated that real terms residual income was obviously *not* the prime indicator of economic performance. One executive complained that four months after the closure of the books he was still unaware of the real terms residual income performance of his unit for the previous year (during which no indication had been available either). He reflected that it was a pity that his bonus depended on real terms residual income, but that he had had to book his family's holidays without knowing whether or not he had earned a bonus for the previous year. How much of an incentive scheme was that?

reduce the adjustments made to financial accounts to a bare minimum of transparently calculated essentials. If real terms residual income is to become the fundamental measurement concept for economic capital creation of an organization (as we believe it should), it must be readily available for periodic reporting within short timetables. As a matter of principle, an organization needs a single prime indicator of economic value creation, and in this regard conventional profit and loss (P&L) measures fall short.

The consequences of generating either excesses or shortfalls on any or all capitals will be dealt with later in the book. For the present, it is sufficient to recognize that the setting of sustainability norms for financial capital and the measurement of actual performance compared to those norms is identical to the MultiCapital Scorecard's treatment of all other capitals.

Before moving on, we must consider the liquidity of the organization as well as its profitability. It is as well to bear in mind that the collapse of organizations is more often due to their running out of funds than their inadequate profitability. It is also a fact that the more statistical adjustments that are applied to the financial results of an organization (however valid the reasons for the adjustments) the more distant they tend to become from reflecting the cash situation of the reporting entity. Sustainable treasury management therefore involves a combination of internal management abilities, operational cash flows, liquid resources, short-term investments, and borrowing capacity. It is extremely context-specific and multistakeholder dependent.

We therefore believe that multiple capital, context-based management offers a benefit to user organizations that escapes many others; namely, the ability to set sustainability criteria that preserve the organization's **effective liquidity**. This vital capital has not been named specifically. However, the powerful combination of stakeholder engagement and identifying vital capitals unleashed by multiple capital, context-based management enables the concept of effective liquidity to be constructed across a broader spectrum of responsible actors and treated as the vital capital that it is and always has been.

Borrowing capacity is one component of effective liquidity. All Western governments (our lenders of last resort) have come to understand between 2008 and 2015 that borrowing capacity should not be taken for granted. Indeed, it may be argued that the whole of the Western world has been salvaged from the brink of successive liquidity crises by the desperate measures of governments to renegotiate and reconfigure their borrowing capacities beyond any limits that would have been considered sustainable some years earlier. As we all know, the result has exacerbated the financial burden that we in the West are placing on our children and theirs. We have therefore in the first decade and a half of the twenty-first century very much exceeded the sustainable limits of our own economic performance and placed the debt burden on future generations.

The MultiCapital Scorecard calls for continuous dialogue with stakeholders to consider and reconsider the mechanisms in place, as well as their continued viability and effectiveness to cope with the liquidity demands that may be placed on them. In many cases this will require an appraisal of the ability of the organization to meet its existing legal agreements for debt repayments as they fall due. As elsewhere under the MultiCapital Score-card, the first question will be: "How much is enough?" That means "How much borrowing capacity is sustainable?" and then "How much interest and repayment of debt are enough to maintain that borrowing capacity at sustainable levels?"

In extending the principles of Context-Based Sustainability to the economic and financial domains, we believe that we are therefore identifying new concepts of stakeholder responsibility that were lurking in the shadows in the era before sustainability reporting stepped into the spotlight. By engaging with stakeholders such as equity holders, lenders, government bodies, suppliers, consumers, and employees and asking what duties and obligations they believe the organization has to them, we are able to formulate new vital capitals and identify limits and responsibilities for producing, maintaining, and managing within them. Whatever its profitability profile,

Application Tips for Organizations Yet to Start Using Real Terms Residual Income

- Treat month-end closures like Grand Prix pit stops; gear up for speed
- Use opening monthly balances for adjustments and charges
- Adopt reliable surrogate indices for price adjustments during the year
- Correct at quarter- and year-end to final indices and exchange rates
- Conduct stakeholder dialogue throughout the year
- Review findings progressively with final review three months from year-end
- Keep all stakeholder meeting notes and workings for audit reviews
- Open dialogue with auditors before embarking on the process

MultiCapital Scorecard Features at a Glance

By extending the Context-Based Sustainability principles to all financial stakeholders in the MultiCapital Scorecard, we believe we have accomplished many advantages that are unique to the MultiCapital Scorecard:

- Triple bottom line sustainability performance in the MultiCapital Scorecard includes all three bottom lines on identical principles showing "How much is enough to be sustainable?" in each case.
- Standards are set in the MultiCapital Scorecard for impacts on all vital capitals in terms that are meaningful to each stakeholder group (monetized when appropriate, nonmonetized when appropriate).
- Financial performance standards include sustainable debt and liquidity performance as well as an adequate return on equity invested. Financial sustainability underpins all other aspects of sustainability performance.
- Progression measurements for impacts that fall short of sustainability norms allow organizations to quantify their progress toward becoming sustainable using the MultiCapital Scorecard.
- Sustainability norms may be determined centrally or by each division, depending on the organization and its multiple contexts. The same applies to trajectory targets. Performance standards are therefore meaningful both to each division and in aggregate under the MultiCapital Scorecard.
- The MultiCapital Scorecard sets stakeholder engagement requirements that include shareholders and lenders. These allow

an organization that is not sustainable in terms of its effective liquidity risks failing all its stakeholders, not just its financial stakeholders. This makes it a vital capital for most if not all organizations, including governments.

In noncommercial organizations, the identity of the equity holders can be less obvious. For example, a college or a hospital that has been funded by (indeed require) stakeholders' expectations to be articulated explicitly, thereby providing a forum to discuss with all stakeholder groups any trade-offs between their respective aims that management has decided for the benefit of the organization and its environment.

- Strategic formulation and annual performance reporting can be undertaken using context-based norms that show which areas of performance are sustainable and how the others are moving toward becoming sustainable at local and consolidated levels.
- Independent assurance is facilitated with the MultiCapital Scorecard as it requires the articulation of sustainability norms and trajectory targets, reporting actual performance against them all.

As a consequence of all the above attributes, we believe that the MultiCapital Scorecard provides the most meaningful basis yet put forward for integrated reporting. It far exceeds the numerical requirements of the IIRC and the Global Reporting Initiative (GRI). The MultiCapital Scorecard is the only process we know that requires the reporting entity to answer the question "How much is enough to be sustainable?" for all material impacts on all vital capitals.

In so doing, the MultiCapital Scorecard takes corporate sustainability reporting from "interesting accounts of selective good deeds" to holistic measurements of the changes required toward enacting the sustainable futures that the world and its people need. This is more than a step change. It may be difficult, but we ignore it at our peril.

bequests over many years has a continuing duty or obligation to those who bequeathed funds in their lifetimes, although trustees have often taken their place in representing the interests of the long-deceased. These trustees represent the equity holders. They usually expect no financial return on the funds invested, but generally have social objectives. Many endowments require the invested financial capital to be maintained, leaving the fruits of the invested capital to be spent.

Charities are a special case. Charitable givers are effectively the continuing equity holders, but they often expect no money in return. They expect their contributions to be put to good use toward the social or environmental aims for which they donated. Some charities have an intention to continue operating for years or centuries to come. Others expect to be liquidated once the original mission is accomplished. The MultiCapital Scorecard provides feedback to all such stakeholders on the extent to which their expectations (financial and nonfinancial alike) have been met in reality.

In both the above cases, lenders will have their dues taken into account in the financial accounts of the entity concerned.

Governmental organizations are funded by their taxpayers—past, present, and future. Their citizenry is therefore the equity holder in all the government does. But how many citizens believe that they are given sufficient information to enable them to judge the stewardship of their governments (elected or unelected)? We argue that the MultiCapital Scorecard is eminently suitable to all organizations, including governments.

The Application Tips box offers some practical tips toward making real terms residual income quickly available after the month-end for monthly reporting. The MultiCapital Scorecard Features at a Glance box summarizes key scorecard features before we move into part 2's worked examples.

PART TWO

MultiCapital Scorecard Reports

CHAPTER FIVE

Case Study: Worked Reports for Company ABC

In this chapter, we seek to illustrate the MultiCapital Scorecard scoring process over a number of years through worked examples of the scorecard with corresponding information on various aspects of the vital capitals and impacts on stakeholders. We present a case study for a hypothetical company. Then, we work through five hypothetical years of change for each of the nine areas of impact for that company. Worked examples introduce you to the suite of MultiCapital Scorecard reports, and show how the MultiCapital Scorecard allows us to monitor sustainability performance and the progression of the implementation process in each impact area, all in comparable terms.

The Case Study

A Big Company (ABC) manufactures, markets, and distributes food products from a single site in a rural setting outside a large city. ABC's supplies come from local produce and from imports. Its markets are mostly regional and are demanding. Some products are exported. ABC has a high profile in its community and its products enjoy a high reputation for fine quality.

It launched a multicapital sustainability project in late 2014. Speaking at the starting point of that project, the ABC president said:

> *Our business is fairly new to the idea that sustainability touches every part of the organization. Some enthusiasts have attempted to become less unsustainable, driving projects and issues with great vigor. Others have just tried to make sure they do the best they can the way they always did. Quality in all we do has always been ABC's aim, including adopting new products and processes in our field of expertise. Our management and our workforce are of the highest caliber and are very loyal, absolutely vital to our business. We have gone through difficult times together and have the team spirit to deal with whatever hits us. We want to be here for the long run and that means being sustainable.*

Still, the company's overall performance statement indicates a varied and inconsistent performance record. At the start of the multicapital project, its impacts on vital capitals register a wide array of scores. However, the president and vice-presidents (knowing there was a strong feeling in favor of sustainable initiatives from people throughout the organization) made firm commitments to adopt sustainability objectives as much as possible in all they do. Thus, nine areas of impact were identified, some (such as workplace safety) broken down into various component-indicators. Initial stakeholder engagement has been undertaken and dialogue is underway on various fronts.

The Company Context

Financial results of ABC have been below expectations, but the company has been profitable. The leaders of ABC have always thought of the company as a good employer. They have set workplace safety as ABC's highest priority alongside its financial objectives.

Understanding the Reports That Follow

This chapter contains reports identifying organization-specific stakeholders, as well as areas of impact and their corresponding sustainability norms and trajectory targets. It also illustrates how performance in the fictitious ABC case might actually be scored and reported using standardized MultiCapital Scorecard templates.

In some cases, sustainability norms shown in the reports are set by the start of 2015, in others the process takes longer and they are introduced later. In each area of impact, the year of the sustainability norm's introduction and of the corresponding trajectory targets are indicated. Each annual MultiCapital Scorecard is presented as if that particular year is complete and its data is available.

After the MultiCapital Scorecard section for ABC, a simplified consolidation or aggregation of three "subsidiaries" is set out in chapter 6. The subdivisions of the group may indeed be legal subsidiaries, but they may also be divisions, regions, brands, or other lines of activity meaningful to the group. This may be as well as, or instead of, subsidiaries.

The MultiCapital Scorecard suite of worked reports for ABC includes the following:

1. Stakeholders and areas of impact
2. Performance reports for each of ABC's areas of impact
3. ABC's MultiCapital Scorecard for each year from 2015 to 2019
4. Five-year bottom line performance summary
5. Group consolidation principles
6. Consolidated MultiCapital Scorecard
7. Consolidated five-year bottom line performance summary

The first four are shown in this chapter, while the remaining three on consolidation are shown in chapter 6. The main features of each report, though, are described in figure 5.1.

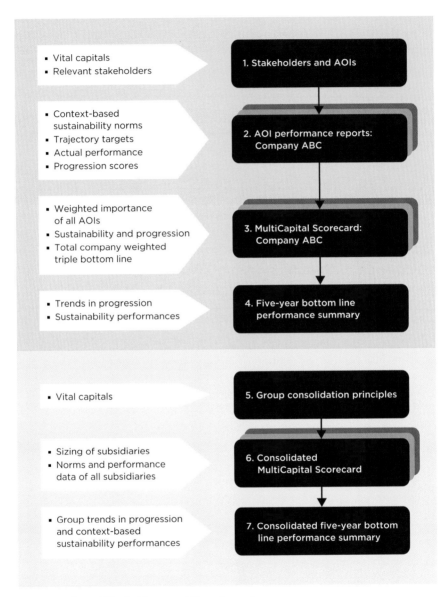

- Vital capitals
- Relevant stakeholders

1. Stakeholders and AOIs

- Context-based sustainability norms
- Trajectory targets
- Actual performance
- Progression scores

2. AOI performance reports: Company ABC

- Weighted importance of all AOIs
- Sustainability and progression
- Total company weighted triple bottom line

3. MultiCapital Scorecard: Company ABC

- Trends in progression
- Sustainability performances

4. Five-year bottom line performance summary

- Vital capitals

5. Group consolidation principles

- Sizing of subsidiaries
- Norms and performance data of all subsidiaries

6. Consolidated MultiCapital Scorecard

- Group trends in progression and context-based sustainability performances

7. Consolidated five-year bottom line performance summary

Figure 5.1. The MultiCapital Scorecard flow of reports.

The Stakeholders and Areas of Impact Report

The stakeholders and areas of impact report for company ABC (see table 5.3) lists all of the company's stakeholders and their associated AOIs with their corresponding vital capitals. It also shows how each group of stakeholders and each AOI align with each of the three bottom lines—social, environmental, or economic. This is an essential report for laying out the overall landscape of the company's obligations to its stakeholders regarding its impacts on vital capitals in a triple bottom line context.

The Areas of Impact Performance Reports

The nine areas of impact that ABC defined sustainability targets for are: living wages, workplace safety, innovative capacity, equity, debt, competitive practices, water supplies, solid wastes, and the climate system. On the pages ahead you'll see each of these AOIs summarized in a two-page report spread.

The report on each spread's left-hand page provides a general overview of the AOI, detailing:

- The stakeholder(s) involved in the specific AOI
- The duty owed to the stakeholder(s) by the company
- The company's self-defined sustainability norm for the specific AOI
- The 2015 starting point
- The rationale for trajectory targets to meet the long-term goal
- The scenario

It is important to note that, true to the spirit of the real world, the future did not always unfold the way ABC had expected it to when setting the targets. The scenario section explains briefly how management reacted to each set of circumstances, interacting with the relevant stakeholders where needed to decide on a way forward for each AOI.

The report on the right-hand page of each spread has two components. The top chart shows how ABC's performance progresses over the five years compared to trajectory targets and sustainability norms. It thereby shows when the company is operating sustainably and when it is not in the given AOI. The lower chart is a single line diagram that reflects the company's corresponding progression scores for the same AOI.

The MultiCapital Scorecard

TABLE 5.1. Overall Triple Bottom Line Performance for Company ABC

	2015	2016	2017	2018	2019
Overall Performance	32%	31%	73%	57%	83%

TABLE 5.2. The Progression Performance Scoring Schema for the MultiCapital Scorecard

NUMERIC SCORE	SCORE DEFINITION
+3	Meeting or exceeding the sustainability norm for the year
+2	Meeting or exceeding the year's trajectory target, but falling short of the sustainability norm
+1	Improving upon the previous year's performance, but not meeting the year's trajectory target, or any year of improving performance, while having no such targets at all (sustainability norms or trajectory targets)
0	Maintaining the previous year's performance, while not meeting the year's trajectory target
-1	A 1-year regression in performance, while not meeting the year's trajectory target
-2	A 2-year regression in performance, while not meeting the year's trajectory target
-3	A 3-or-more year regression in performance, while not meeting the year's trajectory target, or any year of worsening performance while having no such targets at all (sustainability norm or trajectory target)

TABLE 5.3. Stakeholders and Areas of Impact for Company ABC

BOTTOM LINE	STAKEHOLDERS	AREAS OF IMPACT / (CAPITALS)
Social	Employees	Living wage (H)
	Employees and contractors	Workplace safety (H,S,C)
	Consumers, employees, universities, communities, and shareholders	Innovative capacity (H,S,C)
Economic	Shareholders	Equity (IE)
	Lenders	Debt (IE)
	Competitors, customers, shareholders, and communities	Competitive practices (EE)
Environmental	Local community	Water supplies (N)
	Local/regional community	Solid waste (N)
	Global community	The climate system (N)

Capitals Legend:
C = Constructed*   H = Human*   N = Natural
EE = External economic*   IE = Internal economic*   S = Social and relationship*
*These capitals are typically inclusive of intellectual capital, which need not be separately listed.

The MultiCapital Scorecards

After the nine areas of impact have been explained individually, we present the top sheet of the MultiCapital Scorecard. This is what an organization would present annually to its executive committee and at annual stakeholder meetings. This report shows the triple bottom line performance for each year and the overall performance indicator, which reflects the aggregate progression toward the ideal 100 percent (fully sustainable) status. Table 5.1 shows that progression: You can see that ABC makes a very significant improvement over the five years, albeit with many ups and downs.

Readers can see all the individual areas of impact on the MultiCapital Scorecard, as well as annual performance scores and total overall performance for each of the impact areas and each of the three bottom lines. This framework helps management and stakeholders understand areas of shortfall and explore potential areas of resource surplus. As a consequence, action plans can be developed to address any imbalances with corrective action.

Before launching in, it may be helpful to review the progression scoring schema used in assessing performance in the MultiCapital Scorecard (first shown in chapter 3 and repeated here for convenience as table 5.2.).

Living Wage

STAKEHOLDERS: Employees

DUTY OWED BY THE COMPANY: The payment of a living wage to all employees. Livelihoods at a living wage contribute to the formation of human capital in the social bottom line. (Alternatively, wages could be considered contributions to the economic capital of the employees.)

SUSTAINABILITY NORM: All employees are paid at least a living wage.

2015 STARTING POINT: Until now the company has complied with local legal minimum wages ($20,000 per year in 2014). This has recently been shown to be below living wages for those on, or close to, minimum wages for full-time equivalent (FTE) hours for some peer group companies in the region.

RATIONALE FOR TRAJECTORY TARGETS: In 2015 the company will work on establishing the sustainability norm, meanwhile giving a 30 percent wage increase to all staff on minimum wage and to others close to it to bring them all up to a new minimum wage for the company. By early 2016, the company negotiates with employees and unions a sustainability norm and trajectory targets in order to reach it (in real terms) by 2019.

SCENARIO: Trajectory targets and sustainability norms are established in 2016 (including an inflation-adjustment mechanism). A further significant wage increase in 2017 exceeds trajectory targets and is followed by yearly increases to achieve firstly the trajectory targets (2018) and then the sustainability norms (2019).

TABLE 5.4.

	2015	2016	2017	2018	2019
Sustainability Norm (minimum threshold)	—	$35,000	$36,050	$37,132	$38,245
Trajectory Targets	—	$29,061	$32,123	$35,184	$38,245
Annual Wage of Lowest Paid FTE	$26,000	$28,000	$32,250	$35,184	$38,245
Progression Score	1	1	2	2	3

Case Study: Worked Reports for Company ABC

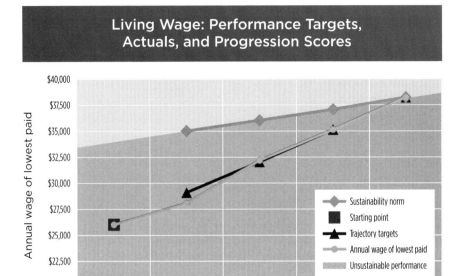

Figure 5.2a. Living Wage: Performance Targets versus Actual.

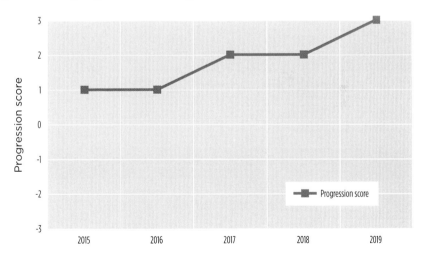

Figure 5.2b. Living Wage: Progression Performance.

Figure 5.2a shows how the trajectory targets and the annual lowest wage tracked against the company's sustainability norm over time, indicating that it was operating unsustainably during most of that five-year period. **Figure 5.2b** shows ABC's progression performance on its living-wage goals over the same five-year period. ABC eventually met its living wage sustainability norm in 2019.

Workplace Safety

STAKEHOLDERS: Employees and contractors

DUTY OWED BY THE COMPANY: To maintain zero fatalities and ensure that operating procedures minimize accidents to all personnel on company work.

SUSTAINABILITY NORM: There are no fatalities, and workplace accidents are below industry and regional norms.

The company has developed a composite index of workplace safety, drawing upon food industry and local peer group accident rates, as well as zero fatalities. A sustainability norm of 100 represents a case in which no employees or contractors suffer fatalities at work and occurrences of injuries and other accidents are at no more than 50 percent of those in peer groups. A score at or above 100 is therefore sustainable; any score below 100 is unsustainable.

2015 STARTING POINT: Workplace safety is a high priority area with a strong track record of progressive improvement. Sustainability norms have been surpassed for a number of years.

RATIONALE FOR TRAJECTORY TARGETS: No trajectory targets have been established as the company has been operating above the sustainability threshold.

SCENARIO: Serious injury to a workplace contractor (ignoring regulations for the use of protective clothing) in 2016 represents a major deviation from a very positive performance trend. New disciplines are introduced to ensure compliance by contractors and employees alike. Good performance is resumed in subsequent years.

TABLE 5.5.

	2015	2016	2017	2018	2019
Sustainability Norm (minimum threshold)	100	100	100	100	100
Trajectory Targets	—	—	—	—	—
Workplace Safety Index	130	70	130	130	130
Progression Score	3	-1	3	3	3

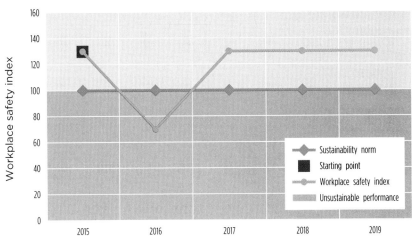

Figure 5.3a. Workplace Safety: Performance Targets versus Actual.

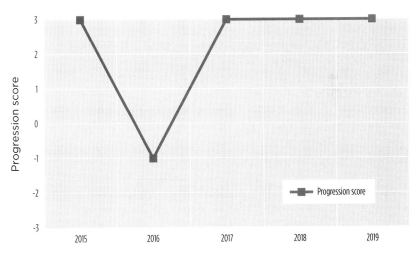

Figure 5.3b. Workplace Safety: Progression Performance.

Figure 5.3a shows the dip in performance in 2016: a one-year regression to unsustainability. Performance in subsequent years is well above the sustainability norm. **Figure 5.3b** illustrates how the MultiCapital Scorecard scoring scheme reflects this series of performances with top scores in all years except 2016, when a -1 score was registered.

Innovative Capacity

STAKEHOLDERS:	Consumers, employees, universities, communities, and shareholders
DUTY OWED BY THE COMPANY:	ABC owes a duty to its stakeholders to maintain its organizational capacity to learn and innovate, its cutting-edge facilities, its research ethos, and its collective ability to renew itself from within. Its innovation needs to empower all employees to harness their creativity in all aspects of organizational life. This includes the development of ecologically, socially, and economically better ways of doing business while maintaining leadership of sustainable brands.
SUSTAINABILITY NORM:	An annual improvement in innovative capacity of 5 percent is thought to be sufficient for long-term sustainable performance.
	The company has developed a composite index of innovative capacity, drawing upon its ranking as an employer of top graduates, employee hours engaged in innovation projects, ideas entering the innovation funnel, projects progressing to implementation, quality of research and development facilities, and collaborative projects run with leading innovators.
2015 STARTING POINT:	The company believes it excels in innovation. However, with competition for qualified talent on the increase, it considers it will find it a tough challenge to increase its composite index scores of 801 at the outset by 5 percent every year.
RATIONALE FOR TRAJECTORY TARGETS:	There is no trajectory target initially as the sustainability norm is being achieved. The sustainability norm of each year increases by 5 percent to give the sustainability norm of the next year. After failure to meet the sustainability norm in 2016, a trajectory target is set up to recover the sustainability norm by 2019.
SCENARIO:	A new organization recruits research and development staff and attracts some of our company's top talent, resulting in lower index scores for 2016 and 2017. The company fails to meet its sustainability norm, despite improving each year on its prior year's score after 2016.

TABLE 5.6.

	2015	2016	2017	2018	2019
Sustainability Norm (minimum threshold)	801	841	883	927	974
Trajectory Targets	—	—	805	889	974
Innovative Capacity Index	801	720	760	860	960
Progression Score	3	-1	1	1	1

Case Study: Worked Reports for Company ABC

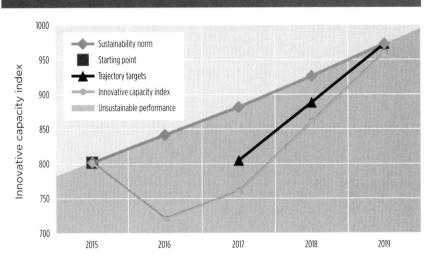

Figure 5.4a. Innovative Capacity: Performance Targets versus Actual.

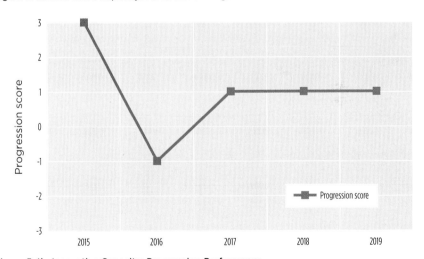

Figure 5.4b. Innovative Capacity: Progression Performance.

Figure 5.4a shows the steep rise in the innovative capacity index that ABC leaders thought would be needed for the business to be sustainable. The sustainability norm is retained throughout the period despite the very poor performance in 2016. Thereafter it can be seen that, despite best endeavors, actual performance improves but fails to meet the trajectory targets throughout the period. **Figure 5.4b** reflects this in the progression scores. The -1 score in 2016 improves to +1 in subsequent years with a return to meeting the sustainability norm apparently within reach for 2020.

The MultiCapital Scorecard

Equity (Shareholders' Funds)

STAKEHOLDERS: Shareholders (equity investors)

DUTY OWED BY THE COMPANY: Providing investors with a return on their capital investment commensurate with the financial return expected of businesses in a similar risk category. Shareholders have stated that 10 percent per year is their long-term threshold. Below this they will withdraw their funding. Market analysis suggests that 10 percent is indeed the opportunity cost of equity capital.

SUSTAINABILITY NORM: A return on shareholders' investment (equity capital) at 10 percent per year is taken as a cost of capital to the net income for each year. Any residual income remaining represents an increase in equity capital: Any deficit indicates the extent to which economic performance falls short of the relevant equity stakeholders' expectations. Zero residual income therefore sets the sustainability norm for the return on equity investors' capital.

2015 STARTING POINT: Annual net income is improving (now 6.5 percent return on the value of invested capital) but residual income is still negative. Management needs to negotiate with equity holders a recovery plan to meet the sustainability norm while paying living wages and investing in research and development.

RATIONALE FOR TRAJECTORY TARGETS: By 2016, residual income trajectory targets are set at -$3 million for 2016; -$2 million for 2017; -$1 million for 2018; arriving at the zero sustainability norm in 2019. This allows for the plans to be accomplished without equity investors pulling out.

SCENARIO: Rationalization of the company's product line focuses on its core competencies, driving innovation into its most profitable products. As a result, profitability increases despite meeting the higher costs of research and development and paying living wages. Trajectory targets are reached each year apart from 2018 as a result of storm damage repair costs. Equity holders see yearly earnings growth (except in 2018) and achieve the required zero residual income in 2019.

TABLE 5.7.

	2015	2016	2017	2018	2019
Sustainability Norm (minimum residual income)	0	0	0	0	0
Trajectory Targets ($m)	—	-3	-2	-1	0
Residual Income ($m)	-3.5	-3	-2	-2	0
Progression Score	1	2	2	0	3

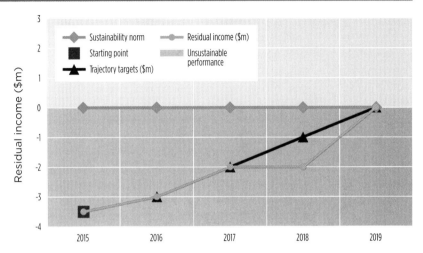

Figure 5.5a. Equity: Performance Targets versus Actual.

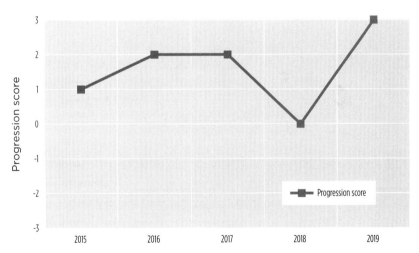

Figure 5.5b. Equity: Progression Performance.

Figure 5.5a shows the negative residual income being earned from the outset. The trajectory targets reach the zero sustainability norm in 2019. Actual performance is in line with the respective trajectory targets in 2016 and 2017, but shows no improvement in 2018. In 2019 ABC meets both its trajectory target and its sustainability norm. **Figure 5.5b** shows the top score being achieved in 2019 and also how the mixed progression toward it is reflected in the MultiCapital Scorecard.

Debt					

STAKEHOLDERS:	Lenders
DUTY OWED BY THE COMPANY:	To ensure operational cash flows comfortably cover the debt-servicing requirements agreed with lenders as well as covering dividend outflows.
SUSTAINABILITY NORM:	Debt service cover of 2 (operational cash inflows at twice the sum of interest and loan repayments required). Lenders renew maturing loans in 2015, based on the management's financial projections of improved profitability and tighter controls of working capital. Together these predicted operational cash inflows over the long term are twice the combined totals of interest and debt repayments; hence the sustainability norm set for 2016.
2015 STARTING POINT:	The company has consistently been generating sufficient funds to pay interest and dividends, but insufficient funds to repay debt at the due date (a long-neglected legal obligation). 2014 debt service cover was 1.1.
RATIONALE FOR TRAJECTORY TARGETS:	In 2016 the company postpones fixed-asset replacement expenditure to reduce borrowing requirements. It also renegotiates with lenders a business and finance plan, rescheduling debt repayments, agreeing to trajectory targets progressively moving toward the sustainability norm by 2020.
SCENARIO:	The reduction in borrowing requirements and improving profitability improve financial performance such that trajectory targets are achieved in 2016 and 2017. The trend is broken in 2018 due to unforeseen borrowing requirements (storm consequences). The trajectory targets are reached again in 2019, with every prospect that the sustainability norm will be accomplished in 2020.

TABLE 5.8.

	2015	2016	2017	2018	2019
Sustainability Norm (minimum threshold)	—	2	2	2	2
Trajectory Targets	—	1.2	1.4	1.6	1.8
Debt Service Cover	1.0	1.2	1.4	1.2	1.8
Progression Score	-3	2	2	-1	2

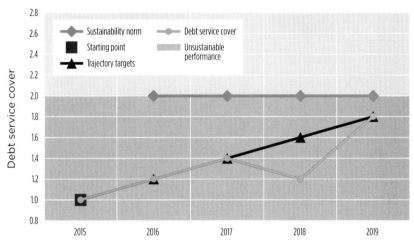

Figure 5.6a. Debt: Performance Targets versus Actual.

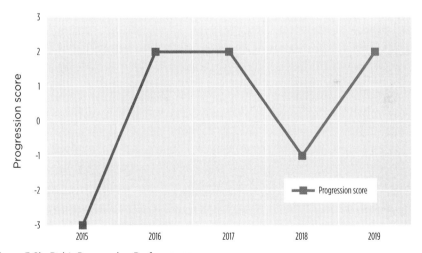

Figure 5.6b. Debt: Progression Performance.

Figure 5.6a shows that despite improvements in performance over time, the company failed to realize its debt service cover goal of 2. **Figure 5.6b** reflects the 2015 starting point with a -3 score, worsening performance, and no plan for improvement. By 2016, the trajectory target is in place and debt service cover meets that target. The progression score therefore jumps from -3 to +2 that year. It then meets its trajectory targets except for the temporary one-year regression of 2018.

Competitive Practices

STAKEHOLDERS:	Competitors, customers, shareholders, and communities
DUTY OWED BY THE COMPANY:	The company will engage in fair competitive practice only; it will do no harm to external economic or social capitals.
SUSTAINABILITY NORM:	ABC will only engage in fair practices globally, as recognized by competitors, customers, and communities. ABC uses third-party assessments of its competitive practices by annual survey in which at least 98 percent of survey respondents (of customers and communities) must rate the company as fair (4) or very fair (5) on a five-point scale in order for its competitive practices to be sustainable.
2015 STARTING POINT:	The company has in the past been suspected of cartel-like behavior. Initial survey results indicate persistent decline and less than 50 percent of respondents giving ABC a rating of 4 or 5. Procurement and sales contracts outside the United States and the European Union have been less subject to legal regulation than those within.
RATIONALE FOR TRAJECTORY TARGETS:	Trajectory targets of improvements of 10 percent per year are believed to be achievable. So trajectory targets of 60 percent in 2016, 70 percent in 2017, 80 percent in 2018, and 90 percent for year 2019 bring the organization to within striking distance of its sustainability norm by the end of the planning period.
SCENARIO:	ABC eradicates all forms of unfair practices by training and setting performance standards for buyers and sellers to establish a strongly held appreciation by stakeholders of ethical values in practice. Application of US and EU laws of personal liability will be adopted internally for ABC's national and international business. Surveys prove slow to show progress in early years, but improve with persistence over time.

TABLE 5.9.

	2015	2016	2017	2018	2019
Sustainability Norm (minimum threshold)	98%	98%	98%	98%	98%
Trajectory Targets	—	60%	70%	80%	90%
Survey Ratings "Fair" and "Very Fair"	48%	55%	65%	80%	93%
Progression Score	-3	1	1	2	2

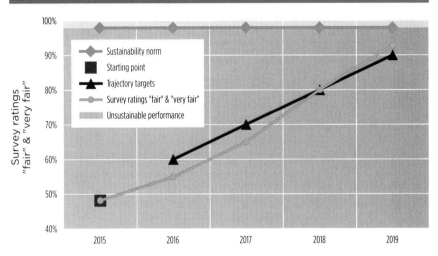

Figure 5.7a. Competitive Practices: Performance Targets versus Actual.

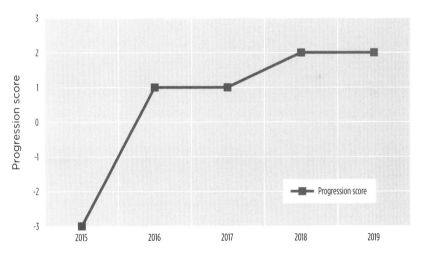

Figure 5.7b. Competitive Practices: Progression Performance.

Figure 5.7a indicates that performance is unsustainable throughout the period. Improvements in 2016 and 2017 remain below the trajectory target. However, by 2018 the trajectory target is met and is exceeded in 2019. **Figure 5.7b** reflects this progressive improvement toward the sustainability norm.

Water Supplies

STAKEHOLDERS: Local community within rainfall catchment area

DUTY OWED BY THE COMPANY: To ensure that the company's water consumption is within its fair share of renewable water resources available.

SUSTAINABILITY NORM: ABC's consumption of water resources does not exceed its fair share of available renewable supplies. This threshold has been calculated as 20 million gallons per year. ABC is aware that this availability and its fair share may fluctuate over time. However, as the company is operating well within its fair share, it need not spend time, effort, or money reviewing the norm with great frequency. The twenty million gallons sustainability norm will therefore be retained until a complete review of all norms is performed after five years.

2015 STARTING POINT: ABC is meeting sustainability norms for water use.

RATIONALE FOR TRAJECTORY TARGETS: The company wishes to keep meeting (or exceeding) the sustainability norm.

SCENARIO: Water use is consistently maintained below the sustainability norm (thereby complying with sustainability norm).

TABLE 5.10.

	2015	2016	2017	2018	2019
Sustainability Norm (maximum threshold)	20,000,000	20,000,000	20,000,000	20,000,000	20,000,000
Trajectory Targets	—	—	—	—	—
Water Consumption (gallons)	12,500,000	13,500,000	12,100,000	14,200,000	11,600,000
Progression Score	3	3	3	3	3

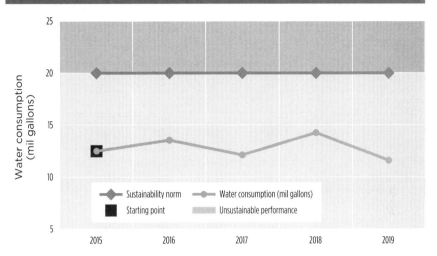

Figure 5.8a. Water Supplies: Performance Targets versus Actual.

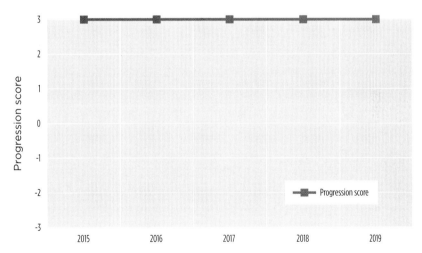

Figure 5.8b. Water Supplies: Progression Performance.

Both charts here simply reflect the fact that water consumption is well within the available limits in all years.

Solid Waste

STAKEHOLDERS: Local/regional community

DUTY OWED BY THE COMPANY: Work toward zero waste to landfill.

SUSTAINABILITY NORM: ABC's deposits of solid wastes to landfill should reach zero.

2015 STARTING POINT: The company has never seriously addressed solid waste issues. Landfill waste is currently running at 1,000 metric tons per year, which is an increase over 2014.

RATIONALE FOR TRAJECTORY TARGETS: A five-year plan with trajectory targets to reach a zero waste to landfill sustainability norm by 2021 is established in 2016. ABC recognizes that its trajectory targets (and sustainability norm) decouple solid waste to landfill from any growth or other change in the nature and size of the company. It nevertheless accepts the challenge.

SCENARIO: The introduction of recycling and composting programs leads to small improvements in 2016 although these fail to meet the trajectory targets. Planned reductions and trajectory targets are achieved in subsequent years, largely as a result of installing a biofuels plant to convert waste to recyclable material.

TABLE 5.11.

	2015	2016	2017	2018	2019
Sustainability Norm (maximum threshold)	0	0	0	0	0
Trajectory Targets	—	900	800	600	400
Solid Waste to Landfill (metric tons)	1,000	950	800	600	400
Progression Score	-3	1	2	2	2

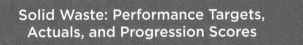

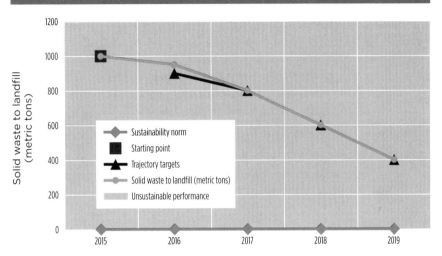

Figure 5.9a. Solid Waste: Performance Targets versus Actual.

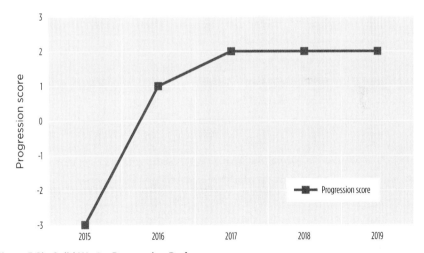

Figure 5.9b. Solid Waste: Progression Performance.

Figure 5.9a shows unsustainable performance in all years. However, once ABC starts to take the solid waste issue seriously, performance improves in 2016, although still not in conformance with the trajectory target that year. **Figure 5.9b** indicates that performance from 2017 on is in line with the trajectory targets, very much on track toward meeting the sustainability norm of zero waste to landfill.

The Climate System

STAKEHOLDERS: Global community

DUTY OWED BY THE COMPANY: To reduce greenhouse gas emissions to a sustainable level as specified in a science-based climate change mitigation scenario.

SUSTAINABILITY NORM: ABC's actual greenhouse gas emissions in any given year should be no more than the sustainable target as specified in a science-based climate change mitigation scenario. By 2015, the company embraces a specific science-based emissions scenario (for example, the Intergovernmental Panel on Climate Change [IPCC]'s representative concentration pathways [RCP] 2.6 scenario) as a standard for what its emissions must be in order to be sustainable by the year 2100.* This 2100 target is close to zero net emissions. As a consequence, ABC chooses to set zero as its own sustainability norm for greenhouse gas emissions, net of offsets and renewable energy credits.

2015 STARTING POINT: ABC's greenhouse gas emissions are 25,000 metric tons per year (the same as 2014), which is an unsustainable level.

RATIONALE FOR TRAJECTORY TARGETS: ABC opts to set itself more aggressive targets than the IPCC RCP 2.6 scenario requires. Management believes it can reach zero net emissions within fifteen years.

The company's trajectory targets are therefore set as a series of annual milestones to reach carbon neutrality by 2030. Individual targets are set for energy consumption reductions at all points throughout the manufacturing and distribution processes. In addition, ABC plans to buy both carbon offsets and renewable energy credits in order to reach zero net emissions with urgency.

SCENARIO: Initial results fall short of the trajectory targets, but lower emissions in 2017–2019 meet the trajectory targets and encourage management in the belief that its trajectory targets will be improved on beyond 2020, toward meeting the sustainability norm by 2030.

TABLE 5.12.

	2015	2016	2017	2018	2019
Sustainability Norm (maximum threshold)	0	0	0	0	0
Trajectory Targets	24,000	23,333	21,667	20,000	18,333
GHG Emissions (metric tons)	25,000	24,100	21,650	20,000	18,300
Progression Score	0	1	2	2	2

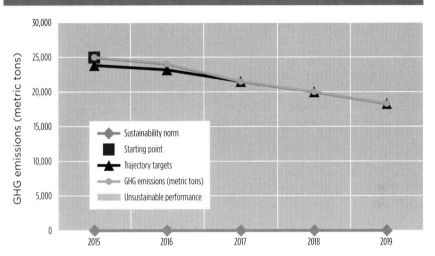

Figure 5.10a. The Climate System: Performance Targets versus Actual.

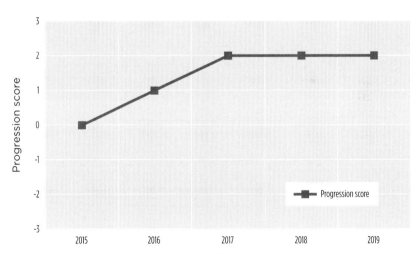

Figure 5.10b. The Climate System: Progression Performance.

Both charts reflect the steady progression of ABC's reductions of greenhouse gas emissions. While emissions reductions remain well short of its sustainability norm of zero emissions, it is nevertheless on course to meet the zero sustainability norm by 2030.

* For more information about the IPCC's RCP 2.6 scenario (and others as well), see https://www.ipcc.ch/pdf/unfccc/cop19/2_knutti13sbsta.pdf.

2015 MultiCapital Scorecard for Company ABC

Vital capitals*

- ■ Natural
- ■ Constructed
- ■ Human
- ▨ Social and Relationship
- ■ Internal Economic—Financial
- ■ Internal Economic—Nonfinancial
- ▨ External Economic—Financial
- ▨ External Economic—Nonfinancial

BOTTOM LINES	AREAS OF IMPACT	CAPITAL IMPACTS	A Progression score	B Weight	C Weighted score (AxB)	D Fully sustainable score (Bx3)	Gap to fully sustainable (D-C)	Area of impact (AOI) bottom line (C/D)	TRIPLE BOTTOM LINE SCORES
Social	Living wage	■	1	1	1	3	2	33%	
	Workplace safety	■ ■ ▨	3	5	15	15	0	100%	92%
	Innovative capacity	■ ■ ▨	3	2	6	6	0	100%	
Economic	Equity	■	1	5	5	15	10	33%	
	Debt	■	-3	1	-3	3	6	-100%	-5%
	Competitive practices	▨ ▨	-3	1	-3	3	6	-100%	
Environmental	Water supplies	■	3	3	9	9	0	100%	
	Solid waste	■	-3	2	-6	6	12	-100%	10%
	The climate system	■	0	5	0	15	15	0%	
	OVERALL PERFORMANCE				24	75	51		**32%**

Note: Areas of Impact shown here are purely illustrative and are always organization-specific.

* Intellectual Capital is typically embedded in most of the others.

Figure 5.11. The MultiCapital Scorecard for year one. The first MultiCapital Scorecard produced by ABC shows the progression scores in each area of impact as earlier indicated on the preceding pages. It also introduces in column B the weighting factors (which are held constant throughout the five-year period). Highest weighting is given to workplace safety, equity, and the climate system. In 2015, good social bottom line performance is undermined by poor performances in the economic and environmental bottom lines.

2016 MultiCapital Scorecard for Company ABC

Vital capitals*

- Natural
- Constructed
- Human
- Social and Relationship
- Internal Economic—Financial
- Internal Economic—Nonfinancial
- External Economic—Financial
- External Economic—Nonfinancial

			A	B	C	D			
BOTTOM LINES	AREAS OF IMPACT	CAPITAL IMPACTS	Progression score	Weight	Weighted score (AxB)	Fully sustainable score (Bx3)	Gap to fully sustainable (D-C)	Area of impact (AOI) bottom line (C/D)	TRIPLE BOTTOM LINE SCORES
Social	Living wage		1	1	1	3	2	33%	
	Workplace safety		-1	5	-5	15	20	-33%	-25%
	Innovative capacity		-1	2	-2	6	8	-33%	
Economic	Equity		2	5	10	15	5	67%	
	Debt		2	1	2	3	1	67%	62%
	Competitive practices		1	1	1	3	2	33%	
Environmental	Water supplies		3	3	9	9	0	100%	
	Solid waste		1	2	2	6	4	33%	53%
	The climate system		1	5	5	15	10	33%	
	OVERALL PERFORMANCE				23	75	52		31%

Note: Areas of Impact shown here are purely illustrative and are always organization-specific.

* Intellectual Capital is typically embedded in most of the others.

Figure 5.12. The MultiCapital Scorecard for year two. In 2016, the deteriorations in workplace safety and innovative capacity resulted in a negative score in the social bottom line. This was largely offset by significant improvements in economic and environmental performance. However, only in water usage can ABC's performance be considered sustainable (scoring 100 percent).

2017 MultiCapital Scorecard for Company ABC

Vital capitals*

- Natural
- Constructed
- Human
- Social and Relationship
- Internal Economic—Financial
- Internal Economic—Nonfinancial
- External Economic—Financial
- External Economic—Nonfinancial

BOTTOM LINES	AREAS OF IMPACT	CAPITAL IMPACTS	A Progression score	B Weight	Weighted score (AxB)	C Fully sustainable score (Bx3)	D Gap to fully sustainable (D-C)	Area of impact (AOI) bottom line (C/D)	TRIPLE BOTTOM LINE SCORES
Social	Living wage		2	1	2	3	1	67%	
	Workplace safety		3	5	15	15	0	100%	79%
	Innovative capacity		1	2	2	6	4	33%	
Economic	Equity		2	5	10	15	5	67%	
	Debt		2	1	2	3	1	67%	62%
	Competitive practices		1	1	1	3	2	33%	
Environmental	Water supplies		3	3	9	9	0	100%	
	Solid waste		2	2	4	6	2	67%	77%
	The climate system		2	5	10	15	5	67%	
	OVERALL PERFORMANCE				55	75	20		73%

Note: Areas of Impact shown here are purely illustrative and are always organization-specific.

* Intellectual Capital is typically embedded in most of the others.

Figure 5.13. The MultiCapital Scorecard for year three. 2017 performance shows significant overall improvement, with all three bottom lines delivering performances above 60 percent. (Note that 67 percent means meeting or exceeding trajectory targets to become sustainable within the agreed-to time scale.) All areas of impact register positive scores in 2017, with only innovative capacity and competitive practices failing to meet trajectory targets.

2018 MultiCapital Scorecard for Company ABC

Vital capitals*

- Natural
- Constructed
- Human
- Social and Relationship
- Internal Economic—Financial
- Internal Economic—Nonfinancial
- External Economic—Financial
- External Economic—Nonfinancial

BOTTOM LINES	AREAS OF IMPACT	CAPITAL IMPACTS	A Progression score	B Weight	C Weighted score (AxB)	D Fully sustainable score (Bx3)	Gap to fully sustainable (D-C)	Area of impact (AOI) bottom line (C/D)	TRIPLE BOTTOM LINE SCORES
Social	Living wage		2	1	2	3	1	67%	
	Workplace safety		3	5	15	15	0	100%	79%
	Innovative capacity		1	2	2	6	4	33%	
Economic	Equity		0	5	0	15	15	0%	
	Debt		-1	1	-1	3	4	-33%	5%
	Competitive practices		2	1	2	3	1	67%	
Environmental	Water supplies		3	3	9	9	0	100%	
	Solid waste		2	2	4	6	2	67%	77%
	The climate system		2	5	10	15	5	67%	
	OVERALL PERFORMANCE				43	75	32		57%

Note: Areas of Impact shown here are purely illustrative and are always organization-specific.

* Intellectual Capital is typically embedded in most of the others.

Figure 5.14. The Multicapital Scorecard for year four. The economic consequences of storm damage in 2018 temporarily set back both equity and debt performances. Meanwhile good progression was accomplished in both the social and environmental bottom lines.

2019 MultiCapital Scorecard for Company ABC

Vital capitals*

- Natural
- Constructed
- Human
- Social and Relationship
- Internal Economic—Financial
- Internal Economic—Nonfinancial
- External Economic—Financial
- External Economic—Nonfinancial

BOTTOM LINES	AREAS OF IMPACT	CAPITAL IMPACTS	A Progression score	B Weight	C Weighted score (AxB)	D Fully sustainable score (Bx3)	Gap to fully sustainable score (D-C)	Area of impact (AOI) bottom line (C/D)	TRIPLE BOTTOM LINE SCORES
Social	Living wage	■	3	1	3	3	0	100%	
	Workplace safety	■ ■ ■	3	5	15	15	0	100%	83%
	Innovative capacity	■ ■ ■	1	2	2	6	4	33%	
Economic	Equity	■	3	5	15	15	0	100%	
	Debt	■	2	1	2	3	1	67%	90%
	Competitive practices	■	2	1	2	3	1	67%	
Environmental	Water supplies	■	3	3	9	9	0	100%	
	Solid waste	■	2	2	4	6	2	67%	77%
	The climate system	■	2	5	10	15	5	67%	
	OVERALL PERFORMANCE		62	75	13				83%

Note: Areas of Impact shown here are purely illustrative and are always organization-specific.

* Intellectual Capital is typically embedded in most of the others.

Figure 5.15. The MultiCapital Scorecard for year five. In 2019, sustainable performance was accomplished in four areas of impact: living wage, workplace safety, equity, and water supplies. In all bar one of the others, performances met the trajectory targets. Innovative capacity improved strongly, but fell just short of its trajectory target. Consequently, all three bottom lines show healthy scores and the overall performance at 83 percent indicates a company making good progression toward becoming sustainable.

Five-year Bottom Line Performance for ABC

TABLE 5.13. The Five-Year Bottom Line in Table Format

	5-YEAR BOTTOM LINE PERFORMANCE—COMPANY ABC				
	2015	2016	2017	2018	2019
Social	92%	-25%	79%	79%	83%
Economic	-5%	62%	62%	5%	90%
Environmental	10%	53%	77%	77%	77%
Overall Performance	32%	31%	73%	57%	83%

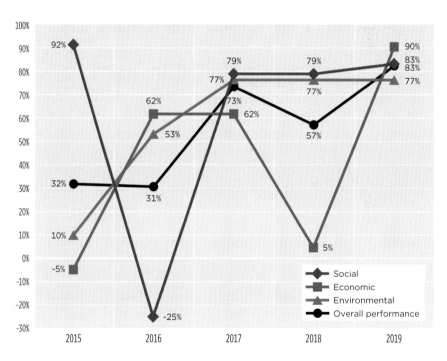

Figure 5.16. The five-year bottom line in graph form.
These five-year runs of triple bottom line performance show significant progression over the period, albeit with some significant setbacks along the way. Perhaps indirectly they also indicate that ABC has developed a resilience over the years to dealing with setbacks while keeping its commitments to becoming genuinely sustainable. Directors of real world businesses and other organizations will recognize the value of having high-level summaries of performance on a single sheet embracing all of the capital impacts they consider to be vital to their prosperity and to their stakeholders' well-being.

CHAPTER SIX

Group Consolidation Principles for MultiCapital Scorecards

The worked examples provided in chapter 5 demonstrate how sustainability norms, trajectory targets, and performance toward sustainability objectives can:

- Be context-based
- Be meaningful to all stakeholders
- Address disparate vital capitals
- Report both sustainability and progression performances
- Be added to reflect the overall performance of an organization

We now wish to show how these principles and practices can be applied to groups comprising multiple divisions of a single organization or subsidiaries with holding companies. In any such collective case, it is likely that a main board (or council or other governance body) will feel a need to address some vital capitals with common goals and metrics. However, the divergent local contexts need to be captured, too.

MultiCapital Scorecard processes allow both of these extreme positions to be embraced. The examples below show how this can be done.

In the following pages, company ABC retains the performance indicators set out in chapter 5. It is, however, joined by two sister subsidiary companies, namely DEF and GHI. For the sake of simplicity, both of the sister companies have 67 percent scores across all areas of impact for all years. The worksheets shown in tables 6.1 to 6.5 set out the consolidation process. This will be familiar to those already accustomed to financial consolidations. But it introduces three ideas that do not necessarily figure in financial consolidations:

Sizing the impacts of divisions of varying dimensions. The examples adopt turnover as the determinant of size and have kept it constant for all years. Sophisticated organizations may develop their own composite metric for the size of sustainability impact, perhaps including a weighting of social, environmental, and economic factors. The MultiCapital Scorecard allows the determinant of size to vary from year to year and therefore to support the evolutionary changes in the shape and nature of the group itself.

Allocating "weighting points" to each division. ABC has been allocated twenty-five weighting points to be assigned to its portfolio of AOIs in any way it likes. In our worked examples, we have allocated this same number to each of the other two companies as well, recognizing that their respective portfolios of AOIs might be larger or smaller than ABC's. This allows each division or subsidiary company to decide whether to have more AOIs at lower weightings or fewer at higher weightings, dependent on their own local contexts. It also acts as a constraint on individual units that might otherwise dominate the consolidation process by establishing overly high importance weightings for multiple areas of impact. (See chapter 3 for additional guidance on scoring and weighting.)

Determining the impacts for which common metrics are appropriate. This is a vital concept. We argue for sustainability norms and the metrics associated with measuring their performance to be established in local contexts. However, there are some circumstances in which a single norm and its metric may be applicable to all parts of the group. The MultiCapital Scorecard allows for such sustainability norms and metrics to be determined centrally for application throughout the group. In the examples, we have selected only two metrics for central determination: equity and the climate system.

Assuming that equity capital is subscribed centrally and represents the basic risk capital funding of all subsidiaries, it is common to all parts of the group (insofar as each is equity financed). We therefore use the working assumption that the opportunity cost of equity capital is common to all subsidiaries. Adopting a common zero residual income goal for all divisions or subsidiaries after charging a common cost of equity capital employed is therefore an appropriate metric for all. Should this not be the case, of course, the group may allow the cost of equity capital to be determined in other, more meaningful, context-based ways.

The climate system is a truly global vital capital. Emissions that impact the climate system contribute in equal measure, regardless of their geographical provenance. We therefore adopt the greenhouse gas emissions trajectory targets and sustainability norms for all divisions, regions, or subsidiaries throughout the group.

Selecting these two centrally determined metrics and areas of impact enables the whole organization to use the same yardstick for impacts on these two vital capitals. Consequently, the global board can respond in detail to stakeholders on performance in these areas of impact. The data collected should therefore be meaningful at both local and global levels. Moreover, the databases of greenhouse gas emissions and of residual income provide rich sustainability data for deeper analysis if the norms are common to all parts of the group. Consequently, the examples below report these two areas of impact separately, as well as incorporating their performances into the triple bottom lines of the MultiCapital Scorecard.

Using these three ideas, the worked examples below allow readers to follow the arithmetic of the consolidation process in detail. Similar principles and processes can be applied to strategic and operational plans as well. Consequently, reporting to the main board and to subsidiary, regional, or divisional boards can show historic performance as well as comparing actual performance against strategic and operational plans in terms meaningful to all. We believe that this is only possible using context-based processes, of which the MultiCapital Scorecard is the most advanced manifestation we know.

The MultiCapital Scorecard

2015 - CONSOLIDATED

BOTTOM LINE	COMPANY	WEIGHTED SCORE	FULLY SUSTAINABLE SCORE	BOTTOM LINE BY COMPANY
Social	ABC	22	24	92%
	DEF	14	21	67%
	GHI	14	21	67%
Economic	ABC	-1	21	-5%
	DEF	16	24	67%
	GHI	20	30	67%
Environmental	ABC	3	30	10%
	DEF	20	30	67%
	GHI	16	24	67%

	COMPANY			BOTTOM LINE BY COMPANY
Company Totals	ABC			32%
	DEF			67%
	GHI			67%

BOTTOM LINE	COMPANY	WEIGHTED SCORE	FULLY SUSTAINABLE SCORE	BOTTOM LINE BY COMPANY
Equity	ABC	5	15	33%
	DEF	10	15	67%
	GHI	10	15	67%
The Climate System	ABC	0	15	0%
	DEF	10	15	67%
	GHI	10	15	67%

Centrally Determined Areas of Impact

TABLE 6.1. Consolidated Annual Integrated Performance Worksheet: 2015

110

Group Consolidation Principles

SIZING

	TURNOVER (MILLIONS)	SIZING	MAX FULLY SUSTAINABLE SCORE	SIZED FULLY SUSTAINABLE SCORE
ABC	$100	33.3%	75	25
DEF	$150	50.0%	75	37.5
GHI	$50	16.7%	75	12.5
Group	$300	100%	225	75

SIZING	SIZED WEIGHTED SCORE	SIZED FULLY SUSTAINABLE SCORE	CONSOL-IDATED SIZED SCORE	CONSOL-IDATED POTENTIAL SCORE	CONSOL-IDATED BOTTOM LINE
33.3%	7.3	8.0			
50.0%	7.0	10.5	16.7	22.0	76%
16.7%	2.3	3.5			
33.3%	-0.3	7.0			
50.0%	8.0	12.0	11.0	24.0	46%
16.7%	3.3	5.0			
33.3%	1.0	10.0			
50.0%	10.0	15.0	13.7	29.0	47%
16.7%	2.7	4.0			
CONSOLIDATED TOTAL		41.4	75.0	55%	

SIZING	SIZED WEIGHTED SCORE	SIZED FULLY SUSTAINABLE SCORE	CONSOL-IDATED SIZED SCORE	CONSOL-IDATED POTENTIAL SCORE	CONSOL-IDATED BOTTOM LINE
33.3%	1.7	5			
50.0%	5.0	7.5	8.3	15.0	56%
16.7%	1.7	2.5			
33.3%	0.0	5			
50.0%	5.0	7.5	6.7	15.0	44%
16.7%	1.7	2.5			

The MultiCapital Scorecard

2016 - CONSOLIDATED

BOTTOM LINE	COMPANY	WEIGHTED SCORE	FULLY SUSTAINABLE SCORE	BOTTOM LINE BY COMPANY
	ABC	-6	24	-25%
Social	DEF	14	21	67%
	GHI	14	21	67%
	ABC	13	21	62%
Economic	DEF	16	24	67%
	GHI	20	30	67%
	ABC	16	30	53%
Environmental	DEF	20	30	67%
	GHI	16	24	67%

BOTTOM LINE	COMPANY			BOTTOM LINE BY COMPANY
	ABC			31%
Company Totals	DEF			67%
	GHI			67%

BOTTOM LINE	COMPANY	WEIGHTED SCORE	FULLY SUSTAINABLE SCORE	BOTTOM LINE BY COMPANY
	ABC	10	15	67%
Equity	DEF	10	15	67%
	GHI	10	15	67%
	ABC	5	15	33%
The Climate System	DEF	10	15	67%
	GHI	10	15	67%

Centrally Determined Areas of Impact

TABLE 6.2. Consolidated Annual Integrated Performance Worksheet: 2016

Group Consolidation Principles

SIZING

	TURNOVER (MILLIONS)	SIZING	MAX FULLY SUSTAINABLE SCORE	SIZED FULLY SUSTAINABLE SCORE
ABC	$100	33.3%	75	25
DEF	$150	50.0%	75	37.5
GHI	$50	16.7%	75	12.5
Group	$300	100%	225	75

SIZING	SIZED WEIGHTED SCORE	SIZED FULLY SUSTAINABLE SCORE	CONSOL-IDATED SIZED SCORE	CONSOL-IDATED POTENTIAL SCORE	CONSOL-IDATED BOTTOM LINE
33.3%	-2.0	8.0			
50.0%	7.0	10.5	7.3	22.0	**33%**
16.7%	2.3	3.5			
33.3%	4.3	7.0			
50.0%	8.0	12.0	15.7	24.0	**65%**
16.7%	3.3	5.0			
33.3%	5.3	10.0			
50.0%	10.0	15.0	18.0	29.0	**62%**
16.7%	2.7	4.0			
CONSOLIDATED TOTAL			**41.0**	**75.0**	**55%**

SIZING	SIZED WEIGHTED SCORE	SIZED FULLY SUSTAINABLE SCORE	CONSOL-IDATED SIZED SCORE	CONSOL-IDATED POTENTIAL SCORE	CONSOL-IDATED BOTTOM LINE
33.3%	3.3	5			
50.0%	5.0	7.5	10.0	15.0	**67%**
16.7%	1.7	2.5			
33.3%	1.7	5			
50.0%	5.0	7.5	8.3	15.0	**56%**
16.7%	1.7	2.5			

113

The MultiCapital Scorecard

2017 - CONSOLIDATED

BOTTOM LINE	COMPANY	WEIGHTED SCORE	FULLY SUSTAINABLE SCORE	BOTTOM LINE BY COMPANY
Social	ABC	19	24	79%
	DEF	14	21	67%
	GHI	14	21	67%
Economic	ABC	13	21	62%
	DEF	16	24	67%
	GHI	20	30	67%
Environmental	ABC	23	30	77%
	DEF	20	30	67%
	GHI	16	24	67%

BOTTOM LINE	COMPANY			BOTTOM LINE BY COMPANY
Company Totals	ABC			73%
	DEF			67%
	GHI			67%

BOTTOM LINE	COMPANY	WEIGHTED SCORE	FULLY SUSTAINABLE SCORE	BOTTOM LINE BY COMPANY
Equity	ABC	10	15	67%
	DEF	10	15	67%
	GHI	10	15	67%
The Climate System	ABC	10	15	67%
	DEF	10	15	67%
	GHI	10	15	67%

Centrally Determined Areas of Impact

TABLE 6.3. Consolidated Annual Integrated Performance Worksheet: 2017

114

Group Consolidation Principles

SIZING

	TURNOVER (MILLIONS)	SIZING	MAX FULLY SUSTAINABLE SCORE	SIZED FULLY SUSTAINABLE SCORE
ABC	$100	33.3%	75	25
DEF	$150	50.0%	75	37.5
GHI	$50	16.7%	75	12.5
Group	$300	100%	225	75

SIZING	SIZED WEIGHTED SCORE	SIZED FULLY SUSTAINABLE SCORE	CONSOL-IDATED SIZED SCORE	CONSOL-IDATED POTENTIAL SCORE	CONSOL-IDATED BOTTOM LINE
33.3%	6.3	8.0			
50.0%	7.0	10.5	15.7	22.0	**71%**
16.7%	2.3	3.5			
33.3%	4.3	7.0			
50.0%	8.0	12.0	15.7	24.0	**65%**
16.7%	3.3	5.0			
33.3%	7.7	10.0			
50.0%	10.0	15.0	20.3	29.0	**70%**
16.7%	2.7	4.0			
CONSOLIDATED TOTAL			**51.7**	**75.0**	**69%**

SIZING	SIZED WEIGHTED SCORE	SIZED FULLY SUSTAINABLE SCORE	CONSOL-IDATED SIZED SCORE	CONSOL-IDATED POTENTIAL SCORE	CONSOL-IDATED BOTTOM LINE
33.3%	3.3	5			
50.0%	5.0	7.5	10.0	15.0	**67%**
16.7%	1.7	2.5			
33.3%	3.3	5			
50.0%	5.0	7.5	10.0	15.0	**67%**
16.7%	1.7	2.5			

The MultiCapital Scorecard

2018 - CONSOLIDATED

BOTTOM LINE	COMPANY	WEIGHTED SCORE	FULLY SUSTAINABLE SCORE	BOTTOM LINE BY COMPANY
	ABC	19	24	79%
Social	DEF	14	21	67%
	GHI	14	21	67%
	ABC	1	21	5%
Economic	DEF	16	24	67%
	GHI	20	30	67%
	ABC	23	30	77%
Environmental	DEF	20	30	67%
	GHI	16	24	67%

	ABC			57%
Company Totals	DEF			67%
	GHI			67%

BOTTOM LINE	COMPANY	WEIGHTED SCORE	FULLY SUSTAINABLE SCORE	BOTTOM LINE BY COMPANY
	ABC	0	15	0%
Equity	DEF	10	15	67%
	GHI	10	15	67%
	ABC	10	15	67%
The Climate System	DEF	10	15	67%
	GHI	10	15	67%

Centrally Determined Areas of Impact

TABLE 6.4. Consolidated Annual Integrated Performance Worksheet: 2018

116

Group Consolidation Principles

SIZING

	TURNOVER (MILLIONS)	SIZING	MAX FULLY SUSTAINABLE SCORE	SIZED FULLY SUSTAINABLE SCORE
ABC	$100	33.3%	75	25
DEF	$150	50.0%	75	37.5
GHI	$50	16.7%	75	12.5
Group	$300	100%	225	75

SIZING	SIZED WEIGHTED SCORE	SIZED FULLY SUSTAINABLE SCORE	CONSOL-IDATED SIZED SCORE	CONSOL-IDATED POTENTIAL SCORE	CONSOL-IDATED BOTTOM LINE
33.3%	6.3	8.0			
50.0%	7.0	10.5	15.7	22.0	71%
16.7%	2.3	3.5			
33.3%	0.3	7.0			
50.0%	8.0	12.0	11.7	24.0	49%
16.7%	3.3	5.0			
33.3%	7.7	10.0			
50.0%	10.0	15.0	20.3	29.0	70%
16.7%	2.7	4.0			
CONSOLIDATED TOTAL			**47.7**	**75.0**	**64%**

SIZING	SIZED WEIGHTED SCORE	SIZED FULLY SUSTAINABLE SCORE	CONSOL-IDATED SIZED SCORE	CONSOL-IDATED POTENTIAL SCORE	CONSOL-IDATED BOTTOM LINE
33.3%	0.0	5			
50.0%	5.0	7.5	6.7	15.0	44%
16.7%	1.7	2.5			
33.3%	3.3	5			
50.0%	5.0	7.5	10.0	15.0	67%
16.7%	1.7	2.5			

2019 - CONSOLIDATED

BOTTOM LINE	COMPANY	WEIGHTED SCORE	FULLY SUSTAINABLE SCORE	BOTTOM LINE BY COMPANY
	ABC	20	24	83%
Social	DEF	14	21	67%
	GHI	14	21	67%
	ABC	19	21	90%
Economic	DEF	16	24	67%
	GHI	20	30	67%
	ABC	23	30	77%
Environmental	DEF	20	30	67%
	GHI	16	24	67%
	ABC			83%
Company Totals	DEF			67%
	GHI			67%

BOTTOM LINE	COMPANY	WEIGHTED SCORE	FULLY SUSTAINABLE SCORE	BOTTOM LINE BY COMPANY
	ABC	15	15	100%
Equity	DEF	10	15	67%
	GHI	10	15	67%
	ABC	10	15	67%
The Climate System	DEF	10	15	67%
	GHI	10	15	67%

Centrally Determined Areas of Impact

TABLE 6.5. Consolidated Annual Integrated Performance Worksheet: 2019

Group Consolidation Principles

SIZING

	TURNOVER (MILLIONS)	SIZING	MAX FULLY SUSTAINABLE SCORE	SIZED FULLY SUSTAINABLE SCORE
ABC	$100	33.3%	75	25
DEF	$150	50.0%	75	37.5
GHI	$50	16.7%	75	12.5
Group	$300	100%	225	75

SIZING	SIZED WEIGHTED SCORE	SIZED FULLY SUSTAINABLE SCORE	CONSOL-IDATED SIZED SCORE	CONSOL-IDATED POTENTIAL SCORE	CONSOL-IDATED BOTTOM LINE
33.3%	6.7	8.0			
50.0%	7.0	10.5	16.0	22.0	73%
16.7%	2.3	3.5			
33.3%	6.3	7.0			
50.0%	8.0	12.0	17.7	24.0	74%
16.7%	3.3	5.0			
33.3%	7.7	10.0			
50.0%	10.0	15.0	20.3	29.0	70%
16.7%	2.7	4.0			
CONSOLIDATED TOTAL			**54.0**	**75.0**	**72%**

SIZING	SIZED WEIGHTED SCORE	SIZED FULLY SUSTAINABLE SCORE	CONSOL-IDATED SIZED SCORE	CONSOL-IDATED POTENTIAL SCORE	CONSOL-IDATED BOTTOM LINE
33.3%	5.0	5			
50.0%	5.0	7.5	11.7	15.0	78%
16.7%	1.7	2.5			
33.3%	3.3	5			
50.0%	5.0	7.5	10.0	15.0	67%
16.7%	1.7	2.5			

TABLE 6.6. Consolidated Group Summary: 2015–2019

CONSOLIDATED SUMMARY							
	2015			**2016**			
Business Units	ABC	DEF	GHI	ABC	DEF	GHI	
	32%	67%	67%	31%	67%	67%	
Bottom Line	Social	Economic	Environ-mental	Social	Economic	Environ-mental	
	76%	46%	47%	33%	65%	62%	
Group		**55%**			**55%**		

CENTRALLY DETERMINED AREAS OF IMPACT							
	2015			**2016**			
	ABC	DEF	GHI	ABC	DEF	GHI	
Equity	33%	67%	67%	67%	67%	67%	
Group		**56%**			**67%**		
The Climate System	0%	67%	67%	33%	67%	67%	
Group		**44%**			**56%**		

Table 6.6. Group consolidated performance in the consolidated summary shows good progression over the five-year period. Total progression scores can be analyzed by company and by triple bottom line component. Because most performance targets are set locally, the choice of areas of impact, as well as metrics and performance standards, are dissimilar and incapable of meaningful analysis at levels below performance progression.

However, the centrally determined areas of impact show a deeper analysis. In this case the areas of impact are equity and the climate system. This enables central management to determine some key areas of impact for the whole group. If they go further and set metrics and norms as well as data collection protocols centrally, they can collect technical detail of performance at a more granular level (for example, metric tons of CO_2e emissions per unit in absolute terms, compared to trajectory targets).

[Note that the group progression scores reflect the working hypothesis that DEF and GHI have 67 percent scores throughout. ABC's impacts therefore account for all of the changes reported in group totals.]

	2017			2018			2019		
	ABC	DEF	GHI	ABC	DEF	GHI	ABC	DEF	GHI
	73%	67%	67%	57%	67%	67%	83%	67%	67%
	Social	Economic	Environ-mental	Social	Economic	Environ-mental	Social	Economic	Environ-mental
	71%	65%	70%	71%	49%	70%	73%	74%	70%
		69%			64%			72%	

	2017			2018			2019		
	ABC	DEF	GHI	ABC	DEF	GHI	ABC	DEF	GHI
	67%	67%	67%	0%	67%	67%	100%	67%	67%
		67%			44%			78%	
	67%	67%	67%	67%	67%	67%	67%	67%	67%
		67%			67%			67%	

PART THREE

Key Issues in the MultiCapital Scorecard

CHAPTER SEVEN

Materiality

Determining materiality involves two main steps: assessing which aspects of performance should be included in measurement, management, and reporting; and addressing what the relative importance of each aspect should be. The criteria for determining financial materiality have been well established, but they prove inadequate for integrated measurement and reporting. The MultiCapital Scorecard breaks new materiality ground in integrated reporting.

In 2014, the UK think tank and consultancy SustainAbility reported that what is really required from this point forward, in the world of organizational transparency, is a kind of one materiality formula or criterion (a single materiality concept appropriate for integrated reporting impacts on multiple capitals).[1] We agree and offer the framework described below.

Capital- and Stakeholder-Based

As we've seen in parts 1 and 2, organizational performance of any kind—financial or nonfinancial—can be measured by comparing an organization's actual impacts on vital capitals to the desired impacts. Defining normative impacts on vital capitals, therefore, is the critically important factor in making materiality determinations for integrated programs or reports.

Such impacts can be unsustainable by either reducing the quantity or quality of vital capitals or by failing to continually produce and maintain them at required levels. Determining materiality, therefore, is about identifying the specific impacts on vital capitals that ought to be addressed by organizations because of the valid stakeholder interests involved.

With few exceptions, stakeholders can and should be classified into groups whenever possible. Such groupings of stakeholders tend to fall into one or more of the following categories: owners, customers, employees, trading partners, communities, and others. Thus, if a company has five million customers, rather than having to interact with every one of them individually, it can formulate a set of duties and obligations that it believes are owed to all of them in common because of their shared customer status. It can then undertake a process to disclose the duties and obligations it feels are owed to customers and invite comments, criticisms, and suggestions from them in response. This form of stakeholder engagement is very important to the MultiCapital Scorecard process.

Not all members of a defined group, however, will necessarily agree with the hypotheses put forward on their behalf. Here it should be clear, though, that at the end of the day it is up to the organization itself, and no one else, to settle on a set of duties and obligations it believes are correct and legitimate for each stakeholder group. This is with stakeholder well-being in mind. Universal agreement on the part of the stakeholders involved is not a requirement. That said, organizations should always be prepared to defend their decisions on such matters, as well as to change their positions in the face of new information or more persuasive propositions. There is no truth with certainty in any of this, only beliefs and claims that survive criticism better than their competitors, at least until something more convincing comes along.

Just as the MultiCapital Scorecard does not dictate the identity of stakeholder groups that are applicable to all organizations, neither does it dictate a definition for the concept of well-being. Instead, it simply requires that organizations identify their own stakeholder groups and the standards of well-being for each group. A well-being definition for customers of a food producer, for example, might be expressed in terms of a science-based state of physical health. Its corresponding duty or obligation owed could be that its products should not put their physical health at risk, and its sustainability norm, therefore, might be that its products should be devoid of harmful ingredients.

Indeed, this is the kind of thinking that is ultimately required in the specification of sustainability norms. Rather than predetermine stakeholder identities, well-being definitions, and sustainability norms, the MultiCapital Scorecard requires that organizations make their own context-based determinations themselves. Whenever possible, the sustainability norms should be science- and/or ethics-based in content.

How Stakeholder Standing Is Established

In the MultiCapital Scorecard, stakeholders acquire their standing in two ways. The first involves considering which individuals or groups are directly affected by an organization's activities. In this case, such individuals or groups receive their stakeholder standing by virtue of the effects an organization is having on vital capitals they (the stakeholders) directly rely on for their well-being. Before they are subjected to such impacts, however, the individuals or groups involved might have no connection to the organization at all. But once the organization's activities affect their vital capitals, they become valid stakeholders. The entity owing the duty or obligation to the valid stakeholder is therefore expected to behave in such a way as to not put the well-being of the stakeholder at risk.

The second way in which stakeholders affect materiality determinations involves considering what an organization's impacts on vital capitals ought to be, whether such impacts are already taking place or not. This includes duties owed by organizations to individuals or groups under the law.

The MultiCapital Scorecard view, then, is that materiality determinations must be made relative to impacts on vital capitals an organization is either (a) already having or (b) ought to be having. Both give rise to duties or obligations to manage one's impacts on vital capitals in some way, the satisfaction of which (or not) constitutes a most basic form of performance and which therefore is fundamentally material for action and management purposes.

Absolute and Relative Materiality

The MultiCapital Scorecard embraces both absolute and relative materiality. Absolute materiality is about whether or not an impact should be considered material at all. Relative materiality deals with the variable priorities and degrees of importance of impacts that have already been determined to be material in the absolute sense. Once an impact has been determined to be material in the absolute sense, it is therefore subject to further qualification in the relative sense. In the MultiCapital Scorecard, three factors pertain to relative materiality in an explicit and quantified manner:

- First, the MultiCapital Scorecard has a *weighting* system that leaders can use to reflect their own organization's views on the relative importance of each AOI. This is not obligatory, but it allows qualitative judgments to be articulated and applied to performance reporting. Our worked examples in chapters 5 and 6 show a range of weightings from 1 to 5: For any organization, the most important impacts are weighted in the scoring system five times as heavily as the least important. This obviously requires subjectivity on the part of the reporting organization, but it is seldom the case that all vital capital impacts are of equal importance. Making the judgment call explicit and making the resulting calculations transparent enables assurers and report users to form their own opinions about the results.

- Next, the MultiCapital Scorecard's scoring system awards full 100 percent *progression* scores for individual AOI performances that meet sustainability norms. More importantly (in the context of the materiality debate), the MultiCapital Scorecard qualifies underperformance according to the effort the organization puts into meeting sustainability norms and trajectory target objectives and their outcomes. For example, not improving, nor planning to improve, attracts a -100 percent score, as does three consecutive years of regressive performance.

    Alternatively, if the organization has its own performance scoring system that plays a similar role, it can feel free to use it within the framework of the MultiCapital Scorecard. Either way, the MultiCapital

Scorecard's performance schema has a qualitative dimension that is reflected in the quantified progression scores.

- Lastly, the MultiCapital Scorecard consolidation process also features a *sizing* mechanism that represents the performance of individual subgroups in a way that is fair and proportionate to their respective sizes. In a business, this sizing metric may be the value of turnover. In an educational institution, it may be the number of students. In a hospital, the relevant size indicator may be the number of patients or beds. In all cases, the consolidated performance scores will reflect the relative materiality of a particular unit or subgroup relative to, and in the context of, the larger group or organization. The MultiCapital Scorecard therefore consolidates meaningful unit scores into meaningful group totals with an explicit context-based sizing mechanism.

How Does This Work in Practice?

The effect of applying these concepts in the MultiCapital Scorecard can be observed in the worked examples in part 2. ABC's very poor social bottom line performance of -25 percent in 2016 (down from +92 percent in 2015) results largely from the workplace injury to a contractor in 2016. Workplace safety has a maximum priority weighting of 5 and a score of -1. Its weighted performance therefore scores -5. At the same time, the loss of innovative capacity (-1) with a weighting of 2 exacerbates the negative score by -2. Despite some improvement (+1) in moving toward a living wage (weighted 1), the social bottom line impact for the year results in a negative performance of -6 compared to a fully sustainable score of 24, or a social bottom line score of -25 percent.

In this total, the MultiCapital Scorecard reflects the perceived importance of the absolute impacts via the weightings assigned to each. Performance is measured with reference to the previous year and to the trajectory targets (as neither of these meets the sustainability norm). The progression toward becoming sustainable is scored against the predefined seven-point scale. Retrograde performance attracts a negative score.

The weighted score of each therefore quantifies in a simple but transparent way both the quality of performance in the year and its importance to the organization and its stakeholders. Both are preestablished before the period of performance is started.

The absolute duties and obligations are met (or not met) for each AOI on its own. However, the qualitative materiality of each one relative to the others is reflected in the MultiCapital Scorecard for reporting purposes. Higher weighted performance scores signify greater progression than lower scores when reporting performance to stakeholders. This aspect of performance measurement is only possible with respect to standards of performance set across all AOIs. The MultiCapital Scorecard sets those standards at the level deemed to be sustainable in each AOI. It then moves on to quantifying qualitative progression materiality for reporting purposes in a novel but transparent way. We now show how to do this in practice.

The Materiality Template

The capital- and stakeholder-based materiality doctrine expounded above gives rise to a tool that we call the materiality template (see table 7.1). This is a tool practitioners can use in the early stages of MultiCapital Scorecard projects to help make materiality determinations.

Focusing on table 7.1's column headings from left to right, the logic of the tool goes largely as follows.

TABLE 7.1. The MultiCapital Scorecard Materiality Template (with Examples Shown)

	ABSOLUTE MATERIALITY		
	Areas of Impact (AOIs)	Corresponding D/Os Exist*	Associated Stakeholder Groups
Social	Product Safety	Yes	Consumers
	Charitable Giving	No	N/A
Economic	Owners' Equity	Yes	Owners
	Provision of Employment	No	N/A
Environmental	Water Use at Plant A	Yes	Local Community
	Water Use at Plant B	Yes	Local Community

* This column asks whether or not corresponding duties or obligations (D/Os) exist for each AOI, by which norms for impacts on vital capitals are defined at levels required to maintain the capitals and ensure stakeholder well-being.

Materiality

The process begins by making absolute materiality determinations, as shown in the first five columns. This in turn starts by identifying areas of impact on vital capitals an organization is either already having or ought to be having in light of duties and obligations owed to stakeholders. This assumes stakeholders have already been identified.

The second column in table 7.1 calls for judgments as to whether or not a duty or obligation exists for the AOIs initially listed. Indeed, not all social and environmental areas of impact will have corresponding duties and obligations associated with them. In such cases, there are no material stakeholders or impacts involved.

The third column calls for identification of the stakeholders associated with each AOI. These are the parties to whom duties and obligations are actually owed, in which case the impacts involved are material.

In cases where impacts do in fact correspond with duties and obligations owed to stakeholders, the fourth column calls for a further determination as to whether or not the actual impacts, if already occurring, are *de minimis* (so minor as to be of no statistical significance). This consideration only applies to impacts on natural capital, since sustainability performance standards for impacts on that type of capital are always expressed in terms of maximum allowable consumption levels. If an actual consumption level is, in fact, insignificantly if not vanishingly small, the risk it poses to the capital involved—and human/nonhuman well-being, alike—is similarly

Impacts are *de Minimis* (Y/N)[†]	Impacts are Material (Y/N)	RELATIVE MATERIALITY		
		Weight	Progression	Sizing
N/A	Yes	OS[‡]	OS[‡]	OS[‡]
N/A	No	N/A	N/A	N/A
N/A	Yes	OS[‡]	OS[‡]	OS[‡]
N/A	No	N/A	N/A	N/A
No	Yes	OS[‡]	OS[‡]	OS[‡]
Yes	No	N/A	N/A	N/A

[†] Applies only to impacts on natural capitals, which unlike other capitals exist only in limited supplies.
[‡] Organization-specific (OS) assignments of values for these variables are made using standardized MultiCapital Scorecard scales.

insignificant or even nonexistent. On that basis, the AOI can be judged to be immaterial in the MultiCapital Scorecard.

In order to make a *de minimis* determination, we propose a test consisting of three steps. First, determine the extent of the impact (how much of the natural capital's carrying capacity is being consumed or destroyed). Second, generalize the impact to a contextually relevant population as if everyone involved were having the same impact. And third, compare the generalized impact to the total carrying capacity of the capital involved (for example, to the total volume of renewable water supplies in a watershed). If the generalized impact is extremely low (for example, <1 percent of the total carrying capacity), the organization's own impact may be considered *de minimis*.

The fifth column is where the final absolute materiality determination is made. If there is a duty or obligation in column two and the impact is not *de minimis* in column four, a material impact exists in absolute terms.

All AOIs that are material in the absolute sense are then subjected to further consideration in the relative materiality section of the template as follows:

- The first qualifier of interest in that section is in column six: weight. This is where organizations can assign different levels of importance or priority to each AOI and for all impacts relative to one another. We suggest use of a simple scale, such as 1 to 5, with 1 being the lowest importance and 5 being the highest. (See chapter 3 for further guidance on weighting.)

- Next comes the progression scoring in the seventh column. The scoring schema we use in the MultiCapital Scorecard quantifies performance impacts on a seven-point scale. The primary purpose of the scale is to distinguish the qualitative aspects of performance in those areas where performance is not sustainable. Positive progression is rewarded with a positive 1 or 2 score, whereas negative progression is discouraged with a -1 to -3 score. These are measures of performance relative to sustainability norms or trajectory targets that have been defined for each AOI, hence the name we give to it: progression performance relative to targets. Here it is important to point out that the methodology and criteria of relative materiality qualifiers are all assigned on a pre-performance scoring basis. They are assigned to individual AOIs as a precursor to calculating and reporting the overall performance of all AOIs in the aggregate, or the performance of the organization as a whole, including its individual bottom line performance.

- The last qualifier of interest in making relative materiality determinations is sizing, the eighth column in table 7.1. The issue here applies only to consolidated reporting of multiple units or divisions. It is used to indicate the order of magnitude each unit should receive in an overall consolidated performance score. Two different units that are otherwise identical in terms of their weight and progression might be very different in terms of the size of the operations they pertain to. One might be for a manufacturing plant with only a hundred employees and the other for a plant with a thousand employees. The larger plant would be given a higher proportion of the total group performance when reporting the aggregate performance of all operations. Metrics for sizing are organization-specific and can be devised as such. Examples of indicators that can be used for this purpose include employee headcount, revenue or turnover, output or units of production, and square footage or facility size. In the MultiCapital Scorecard, it is up to each organization to choose its own sizing scale.

In sum, materiality determinations in the MultiCapital Scorecard are made in both absolute and relative terms. Absolute determinations are binary and result in decisions about whether or not to include specific AOIs in a scorecard at all. Relative determinations are then made for those AOIs deemed to be material, in which case qualitative judgments about them are also made.

CHAPTER EIGHT

Intangibles

Historically, accounting focused on the stewardship of tangible assets. Economic capital invested by shareholders or owners was shown on balance sheets as a liability due to the investors. The funds invested were represented by the land, buildings, machinery, raw materials, and finished goods the business required to conduct its business: all tangible assets. But tangible assets also included the surplus cash and bank balances, as well as accounts receivable from customers. Tangible liabilities include debts payable to lenders as well as payments still to be made to suppliers of goods and services.

As shown in figure 8.1, the balance of net tangible assets represented more than 80 percent of the market value of the businesses quoted on the New York stock exchange in 1975 (that is, the S&P 500). The same was true of the London stock exchange. Financial accounting therefore captured the lion's share of the assets underpinning the market value. Intangible assets, representing brand values, reputation of the firm, organizational arrangements, communication capabilities, know-how, relationships, and people were often recognized in words, but not in mainstream accounting data.

Since they all added up to less than 20 percent of market value, it was understandable (if not excusable) that they were the Cinderella assets: not invited to the accountants' ball. It would be quite unfair to accuse the financial accounting data of being the ugly sisters. However, as things have turned out forty years later, they have been shown to be completely inadequate to represent the true values that companies have. Despite this, they retain an inordinate dominance of reporting data. As figure 8.1 demonstrates, intangible assets now represent more than 80 percent of corporate values, leaving tangible assets accounting for less than 20 percent. This is not just a US or UK phenomenon; the pattern is found around the world.

The historic focus on tangible assets is therefore an anachronism. If 80 percent of the value of an organization is represented by intangible assets, leaders seeking to create sustainable value need to understand more about how and where that 80 percent is created and what is needed to maintain and grow it. In other words, we need to resume the search for Cinderella. Hitherto, financial accounting has been keeping her out of sight.

But at least one accounting institution, the London-based Chartered Institute of Management Accountants (CIMA), is calling for change. In its June 2015 issue of *Financial Management*, CIMA chief executive Charles Tilley declared:

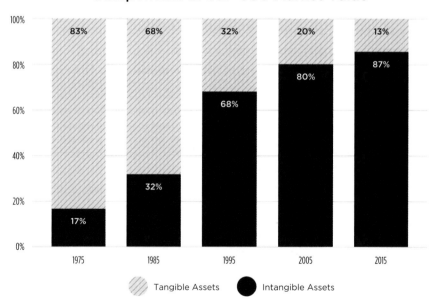

Components of S&P 500 Market Value

Figure 8.1. Components of S&P 500 market value. Tangible assets declined from 83 percent of market value to 13 percent over forty years. Image courtesy of Ocean Tomo, LLC.

CIMA believes it's vital to recognize the growing importance of intangible assets as a precondition of reaching good judgments on value generation. . . . The need for this change in outlook is becoming ever more pressing. It's time for commercial and political leaders to push this issue to the top of their agendas.[1]

It will be clear to readers who have followed the text to this point that the MultiCapital Scorecard addresses many elements of carrying capacity that fall into the intangible asset category. By engaging with stakeholders and asking them what they consider to be the duties and obligations the organization owes them, it provides a structured framework for listening to voices from its own context(s). Stakeholders tend to focus on impacts, and this informs management about the underlying capitals on which their performances impact.

In a world about to be overrun by Big Data, there will emerge new metrics and new answers to the questions the leaders ask. The multinational accounting and auditing firm PwC estimates that only 0.5 percent of data available is currently analyzed.[2] Some of the difficulties in identifying metrics and capturing information in ways that are open to verification will disappear if users ask the right questions. Answers will evolve over time and under challenge from users, peer groups, and auditors.

In this chapter we will look more specifically at two sorts of intangible assets: brands and reputations.

Global Brand Values

Brands are classified by financial accounting standards as intangible assets, but only once they have been bought or sold. A brand that has been built up from within the organization is not allowed by the international rules to appear on the balance sheet. All costs of building such brands have to be written off to expenses as they are incurred. Moreover, increases in the valuation of brands cannot be reflected in the accounts until they are sold.

Financial accounting standards therefore consider it is better to be precisely wrong than approximately right. Precisely wrong, because the rules have been dictated by extreme conservatism and anachronistic concepts of where real value lies. It is obvious to even casual observers that many home-built brands are the most valuable assets their companies own, but still they cannot be valued in financial accounts. Accuracy trumps relevance.

This means that brand accounting data is meaningless when organizations seek to manage brand value creation. In 2014, *The Economist* estimated that the top ten brands in the world were worth roughly $700 billion in 2013—an asset almost entirely home grown, and therefore appearing on nobody's balance sheet.

Some accountants ask how it is possible to separate the values of the brands from the know-how required to make the product or service, the facilities in which they are produced, and the customers and consumers who buy the end product. There are multiple capitals involved in creating, growing, and developing a brand.

But help is at hand. The MultiCapital Scorecard has developed ways of measuring performance across multiple capitals without monetizing that which does not lend itself to monetization. By identifying the vital capitals that comprise the brand (human, constructed, natural, social and relationship, and economic) while setting norms for their continued future existence and measuring performance against each, it is possible to take a quantified in-depth approach to brand value management. Each aspect of each brand's vital characteristics can be identified. Each of these can then be measured (in financial or nonmonetary terms at the firm's discretion) with normative impacts specified and performance measured against each.

External corroboration of some component parts of the marketing mix (traditionally the four Ps of product, place, promotion, and price) has been best practice for decades. For example, market shares, price differentials, distribution patterns, promotional effectiveness, and consumer perceptions have all been available from independent agencies. However, bringing them all together with innovation to establish a multicapital approach to managing each brand in a holistic manner, incorporating environmental, social, and economic aspects, is a property of the MultiCapital Scorecard that we have not seen elsewhere. Introducing the yardstick of asking what is needed to make the brand sustainable in each of these dimensions focuses attention on the future needs of clients and consumers and society in general. The world will become aware of constraints that many simply choose to ignore today.

This brings multicapital integrated thinking to the cutting edge of strategic action. It is, of course, an emerging discipline, and implementation will no doubt raise areas for improvement. Again, better to be approximately right than precisely wrong.

Whereas the MultiCapital Scorecard attends to the component parts and brings them together to reflect their sustainability or progression toward becoming sustainable, it does not necessarily reflect the totality of the brand's financial value. Indeed, the MultiCapital Scorecard explicitly does not need to monetize any nonfinancial vital capitals. Valuation of intangible assets is always a contested art form. But various approaches to brand valuation that are now undertaken show a convergence of valuations, albeit with certain margins of error. This valuation exercise can be conducted in parallel to the MultiCapital Scorecard, which itself focuses on the sustainability of the carrying capacity of the capitals concerned in metrics most appropriate to each.

In a world in which tangible assets represent less than 20 percent of a company's market valuation, is it not time we started to work with approximations for the values of intangibles that account for the other 80 percent? How else can we be said to be protecting and optimizing financial returns from our most valuable assets? The financial performance of the entity depends on establishing both valid valuations of capital employed and valid income streams, neither of which can be provided from the financial accounting standards applied today. Moreover, any framework for valid brand financial performance comparability should not distinguish between purchased brands (for example, Unilever's Ben & Jerry's) and their home-grown brands (for example, Unilever's Magnum).

To compound their errors (albeit with impeccable consistency), accounting rules for managing purchased brands prevent recording any increases in their values. Again, this results from "conservative" principles that deny where real financial brand value is created, preferring to sweep the whole issue under the carpet under the guise of conservative undervaluation. This means that the real value increases of purchased brands remain the elephant in the room that does not feature in "value creation" strategies. Meanwhile, the great hairy mammoth that is not even allowed into the room (that is, the $700 billion worth of home-grown brands) should now be actively encouraged in. The MultiCapital Scorecard opens the door wide enough to let them all in: elephants and mammoths alike! Whether or not financial value is ascribed to brands, the MultiCapital Scorecard treats them equally, be they home grown or purchased.

Denying the capital value of brands and ignoring the flows needed to sustain that value cannot be condoned simply for the convenience of the accounting profession. Sustainable performance measurement requires relevance to trump precision. Here again, it is better to be approximately right than precisely wrong.

How Does the MultiCapital Scorecard Work for Brands?

Traditionally, performance measurements in divisionalized organizations were structured around legal entities that operated in nation states. Many decisions were local. Procurement and distribution were controlled locally.

Now, thanks to globalization, brand management is increasingly international, with key strategic decisions taken centrally for all markets. The brand's personality dictates many of the values that must be applied to procurement, design, storage, and distribution, all of which used to be locally controlled. As more brand personalities take on the values associated with sustainable business, it becomes ever more important to ensure those brand values are being practiced all around the world. Indeed, the international integrity of the brand depends on the environmental and social attributes of the brand being applied appropriately in each local context. Sustainable global branding cannot be managed by monitoring the economic aspects of performance alone. Every aspect of the marketing mix, including the social and environmental impacts, needs to be taken explicitly into account.

Therefore, it is possible to set up a MultiCapital Scorecard as the performance measurement process for the core brands across a global business or other organization. Some relevant vital capitals, metrics, and norms may be decided centrally and applied globally. Note that the MultiCapital Scorecard adopts the metrics most appropriate for each capital. For example, standards for greenhouse gas norms can be expressed in terms of metric tons of CO_2e (carbon dioxide equivalent). Return on capital invested, for its part, may be set centrally as residual income in local currency—after applying, say, a 10 percent weighted average cost of capital—and applied across the world. Others can be determined locally to ensure their relevance, local contexts, and most appropriate units of measurement. These may be shaped centrally with local discretion as to the nature of the duty and the metrics adopted. This would allow maximum use of existing local data sources. The consolidation process can be operated globally. The MultiCapital Scorecard will deliver meaningful results to global brand management as well as to local stakeholders.

But to do this fully (to measure both financial and nonfinancial brand performance) brand valuation needs to be undertaken at the outset of the exercise and renewed periodically as the ongoing reporting process proceeds. Without this brand valuation component, it will always remain impossible to determine the economic performance of the brands in question. Value creation (and destruction in the case of declining brands) cannot simply assume that adequate inputs result in effective outcomes without external corroboration of the value progression of the brands themselves. Moreover, the income flows required to be earned on brands that are declining in value should not be the same as the income required from brands that are investing and generating real economic capital growth. This truism is obvious when applied to tangible assets. Positive capital growth compensates for less strong income streams. We now need to develop the thinking and the tools to apply it to intangibles such as brands.

We argue that the MultiCapital Scorecard makes two significant contributions to ensuring that this can happen:

- The MultiCapital Scorecard asks the sustainability sufficiency question of nonfinancial capitals and nonfinancial impacts alike within a single, meaningful conceptual framework. This enables all organizations to explore and rank their impacts on all the vital capitals that concern them and their stakeholders. In the worked examples provided in chapter 5, we show how the innovative capacity (composed of a mix of nonfinancial capitals that may be critical to the brand's performance) of ABC might be dealt with without monetization.
- And, the MultiCapital Scorecard is entirely capable of incorporating monetized values of brands (or other intangibles) into the financial

sustainability performance measurements as and when valuation techniques become adopted.

This would allow Unilever to compare performance of global purchased brand such as Ben & Jerry's (collecting performance data from all thirty-six countries in which they operate) on a like-for-like triple bottom line basis with Magnum (a home-grown brand that operates in perhaps one hundred countries). Once the mind-sets of all managers, leaders, and directors of such global brands have become driven by truly multicapital values, we believe it will become second nature to require the MultiCapital Scorecard (or something similar) to be the reference framework for performance throughout their organizations. Indeed, early pilots of the MultiCapital Scorecard are already underway at a handful of companies including Ben & Jerry's and Agri-Mark, Inc. (aka, Cabot Creamery Cooperative), two large dairy food producers in Vermont.

As with many other areas of innovation arising from the implementation of the MultiCapital Scorecard, the adoption of new norms means that the old reference points calculated under old norms become incomparable and outdated. Therefore, calculating the increases or decreases in the financial values of brands or other intangible assets raises the question of whether the old standards remain valid (for example, return on capital employed). Since our current accounting practices turn blind eyes to them all, income statements (which most users still consider to reflect the financial truth) remain indifferent to either increases or decreases in their values. Indeed, in the case in point, invested capital is distorted (understated usually), and the income stream is distorted as well by writing off as losses the costs of building brands and then not reflecting the value created by good brand management.

Once we recognize that there is value being created in holding or building these capital assets (or value destroyed in their decline, aging, or mismanagement), we should recognize and reflect those value changes in the financial results of the organization. It is of course true that the gains or losses have not been "realized" until the asset concerned is bought or sold, but that is a mere accounting technicality relative to the scale of the misstatements involved during their period of management. Just as holding tangible assets (such as shares) can create losses or gains, so it can be the case, too, for intangibles. The financial "conservatism" that prevents their gains from being booked (but insists on losses of purchased brands being recorded) results in a biased system. That may protect shareholders' financial capital from being overstated, but only at the cost of possible massive understatements of economic gains made (albeit not realized).

In multistakeholder accountability terms, the old accounting ideas of financial conservatism skew the system and therefore the outcomes of performance reports. It is not the purpose of this book to propose a completely new framework for financial accounting, but suffice it to say that the current framework is severely unfit for the purposes to which stakeholders and society in general need to use it. This is why Warren Allen, former president of the International Federation of Accountants, declared: "The present reporting system is broken."[3]

It should come as no surprise, therefore, that CIMA (which has linked up with the American Institute of Certified Public Accountants to form Chartered Global Management Accountants—CGMA) is taking a stand to value intangibles. Management information has to respond to the demands of the context. Management accountants need not be constrained by the distortions or constraints of financial reporting. In Larry Hirshhorn's terms, CIMA feels itself authorized to work on treating intangibles as real assets as part of the developmental structure of the accounting profession.

CGMA's support of the need to move toward sustainable futures will therefore be underpinned by the recognition of where real value is being created and where it is being destroyed. Responding to this question is far more important to the twenty-first century world than the protection of archaic accounting concepts born of the industrial revolution for a purely financially oriented audience. We wish all strength to the arm of the CGMA that is addressing these fundamental issues. Meanwhile, we expect the adoption of the MultiCapital Scorecard in its nonmonetized sustainability performance mode to prepare enlightened users for futures in which brands and other intangibles stand up to be counted in financial terms, too.

Reputational Capital

Just as individual brands have economic value so do organizations themselves have intangible value that goes beyond the sum of their component parts.

Reputation consultant Simon Cole[4] has identified corporate reputation as a component of the difference between quoted companies' market capitalizations and their underlying net asset values. As he wrote in 2012:

> *Company reputations are, as many already believe, real, present and often very substantial assets. Their presence is considerable in both the UK and the US where they rank among the most important repositories of value for listed companies. As of 1 January 2012 they accounted for close to 26% of the total market capitalization of the S&P500, US$3,190bn of shareholder value. At the same time they were delivering US$770bn of value across the FTSE100.*[5]

The *Fortune's* "World's Most Admired Companies" studies used by Cole in his analysis capture perceptions of a broadly comprehensive set of factors judged to be among the principal components of corporate reputation. These constitute the basic makeup of each company's reputation and are presented in the form of quantitative measures of the strength of perceptions of the following dimensions:

- Quality of management
- Innovation
- Quality of goods/products and services
- Community and environmental responsibility (UK)/social responsibility (US)
- Financial soundness
- Long-term investment value
- Use of corporate assets
- Ability to attract talent (UK)/people management (US)
- Quality of marketing (UK)/global competitiveness (US)

The work done by Cole on what he calls "the reputation dividend" identifies a strong correlation between reputation and market values of quoted companies. Of course, other organizations also have reputational capital, but in the absence of market prices of their shares, it is more difficult to capture and analyze. He concludes that the principal source of value creation for corporate brands derives from investors rather than from customers. For nonquoted companies and other organizations, this can be interpreted as meaning that the reputation of the entire entity is of greater significance than the value of the "brands" of any or all of its individual products or services.

In any case, only three of the nine component parts of reputation constitute the financial element of reputational capital: financial soundness, long-term investment value, and use of corporate assets. The other six are nonfinancial. The MultiCapital Scorecard is eminently suited for managing this constellation of capitals and the impacts on them.

Indeed, in the absence of the kind of actual data provided by the Multi-Capital Scorecard, it is clear that investors still try to estimate performance in nonfinancial arenas. This means that reputation (a very significant capital asset) is informed by the plethora of unstructured, uncoordinated, and possibly inconsistent corporate sustainability reports currently issued from company to company. These are mostly context-free and answer no question in particular. Nevertheless, reputation is positively correlated to market value of the entity. In other words, the interpretation by investment analysts of the sustainability performance of major corporations probably has as a bigger impact on the financial valuation of businesses than any other single factor.

Without falling into the trap of accepting that all else pales into insignificance in the light of this phenomenon, we venture to suggest that Simon Cole's analysis does offer a "business case" for addressing reputation in the best way possible.

CHAPTER NINE

Other Key Issues

In previous chapters, we have dealt with the principles that underpin the MultiCapital Scorecard, its origins in Context-Based Sustainability, and the mechanics of the integrating framework that incorporates financial performance and progression. In this chapter's sections, we'll turn our attention to a number of key issues that arise in many implementations:

Integrated Reporting <IR>: In this section, we summarize the state of the art of reporting on performance across multiple capitals. We reflect on how the MultiCapital Scorecard meets the emerging international requirements and where it goes beyond them.

Shortfalls and Surpluses: Here we discuss the interpretation of exceeding or falling short of performance targets in the MultiCapital Scorecard and explain how to use it to shape strategic sustainability aims.

Double-Loop Learning: This section emphasizes the importance of the double-loop review cycle in continual improvement, explicitly framing the periodic questioning of all aspects of the process to promote learning.

External Assurance provides new eyes to feed into the periodic reviews. This section also explains how the MultiCapital Scorecard helps management, assurers, and report users by setting explicit norms.

Integrated Reporting

The concept of integrating economic, social, and environmental perfor-mance dates back more than three hundred years.[1] However, the practice of integrated reporting is still embryonic.

One of us, Martin Thomas, argued in *New Eyes* that by 2050 it would be the norm for organizations of all sorts to be reporting impacts on their triple bottom lines.[2] The other, Mark McElroy, has argued persistently since 2008 that only context-based norms can provide meaningful sustainability report-ing. Moreover, the United Nations Environmental Programme (UNEP) made an unambiguous call in 2015 to all reporting standards/guidance bod-ies (such as the Global Reporting Initiative, or GRI, and the International Integrated Reporting Council, or IIRC) to adopt Context-Based Sustainabil-ity principles.[3] We therefore fully expect the MultiCapital Scorecard (or its successors) to frame the developments that will become best practice for the decades ahead.

But that leaves us for the present in a state of liminality; that is, in a tran-sitional state between a certain past of financial primacy and an uncertain future of context-based multicapitalism.

Four major influences on sustainability management and performance measurement (integrated or otherwise) have been the GRI, the IIRC, *One Report* (by Robert Eccles and Michael Krzus), and UNEP.[4] We will consider each in turn and summarize how the MultiCapital Scorecard meets their demands. We will also attempt to explain key areas of conflict and any aspects in which the MultiCapital Scorecard goes beyond the requirements of these four frameworks for reporting.

In addition to the above, two significant new books were published in 2015, each casting new light on the <IR> theme: *The Integrated Reporting Movement: Meaning, Momentum, Motives, and Materiality*, also by Robert Eccles and Michael Krzus (with significant support from Sydney Ribot), and *Six Capitals, or Can Accountants Save the Planet?*, by Jane Gleeson-White. Both of these books offer deeper insight into integrated reporting, and so each is considered below as well in the context of integrated reporting.

The Global Reporting Initiative (GRI)

The Global Reporting Initiative set out with the ambitious purpose of providing a set of data definitions within a reporting framework that would allow organizations of all sorts to report to stakeholders on their sustainability performance. GRI's first set of detailed requirements was published in 2002; their most recent at the date of writing was G4 as released in May 2013.[5]

Our main objection to GRI has been and remains its persistent inability to recognize in practice the importance of incorporating context into sustainability reporting. This failure in practice is despite the fact that GRI has for many years espoused the importance of "sustainability context" in principle, as a vital concept for any meaningful sustainability measurement. Furthermore, GRI has consistently awarded its highest accolades to organizations that completely ignore context in their reporting. It is impossible for us to ascribe this omission to an oversight, since GRI has received many notifications and expressions of concern about it over the years (including from the Sustainability Context Group, a community of interest) to point out the omission. Indeed, proposed draft wordings, too, have been put forward to GRI; all to no avail.[6]

So, in terms of being context based, the MultiCapital Scorecard is more compliant with the basic principles of GRI than GRI is itself. The MultiCapital Scorecard requires organizations of all sorts to assess their impacts on vital capitals and to set related standards or norms for their own performance to be sustainable in their own contexts. Thus, organizations identify their sustainability context in order to define meaningful standards of performance for each material area of impact and then measure, manage, and report their performance accordingly.

The MultiCapital Scorecard is fully supportive of organizations that have implemented GRI, but the MultiCapital Scorecard does not require GRI as a prerequisite of meaningful sustainability management. We consider that the conceptual integrity and principles of the MultiCapital Scorecard are more important to the understanding of what sustainability requires of the organization than context-free GRI compliance can ever be.

We conclude therefore that, up to and including G4, GRI has failed to meet its own objectives. We believe that GRI needs to incorporate the MultiCapital Scorecard or some other meaningful context-based approach if it is to win the confidence it will require to make sustainability reporting meaningful within and beyond organizations' boundaries.

The International Integrated Reporting Council (IIRC)

In 2010, GRI joined several other forces for change to give birth to the International Integrated Reporting Council. Prominent among the other forces for change parenting the IIRC was the group known as A4S (Accounting for Sustainability), sponsored by Charles, Prince of Wales. For its part, GRI explains its participation in launching the IIRC as follows:[7]

> As one of its co-conveners, GRI has been involved with the International Integrated Reporting Council (IIRC) since its inception in 2010. . . . GRI and IIRC signed a new Memorandum of Understanding in March 2015, which included the following:
>
> > GRI and IIRC work together as strategic partners. They share a vision for the evolution of corporate reporting. . . . Both organizations recognize the importance of corporate reporting in promoting sustainable development. GRI and the IIRC acknowledge the complementarity of their respective roles, on the basis that sustainability reporting is central to integrated reporting.

Importantly, the IIRC distinguishes integrated reporting from sustainability reporting on the grounds that it (integrated reporting, or <IR>) is about value creation rather than sustainability. GRI only reinforces this view in its G4 sustainability reporting guidelines when it says:[8]

> Sustainability reporting is a process that . . . combines long term profitability with social responsibility and environmental care . . . reflecting positive and negative impacts.

That definition clearly includes all three parts of the triple bottom line. GRI continues:

Integrated reporting . . . aims primarily to offer an organization's providers of financial capital with an integrated representation of the key factors that are material to its present and future value creation.

This suggests that financial value creation is <IR>'s main focus and not integrated financial/sustainability performance reporting at all. Indeed, the GRI document goes on to distinguish between integrated reporting and sustainability reporting, as if they are by nature or in essence fundamentally different as follows:

Integrated reporters build on sustainability reporting foundations and disclosures in preparing their integrated report. Through the integrated report, an organization provides a concise communication about how its strategy, governance, performance and prospects lead to the creation of value over time.

Worthy of note here is that there is no suggestion from the IIRC (or GRI, for that matter) of how to determine how much value needs to be created or maintained. The MultiCapital Scorecard is clear that this question is answered by referring to the needs of all stakeholders in sustainable futures.

And just when it seems to become clear as to how both the IIRC and GRI are framing their definitions, GRI goes on to say:

Although the objectives of sustainability reporting and integrated reporting may be different, sustainability reporting is an intrinsic element of integrated reporting.[9]

We fail to find good reasons for the nuanced differences between sustainability reporting and integrated reporting articulated above. In all cases, the key issue that performance measurement and reporting should address is: "How much is required for performance to be sustainable?" How the impact is classified into social, environmental, or economic categories is of secondary concern. Indeed, performance (integrated or otherwise) is fundamentally a function of impacts on vital capitals relative to sustainability norms. This is true for all forms of performance (financial and nonfinancial alike) whether acknowledged by GRI and the IIRC or not.

By comparing actual performance to norms, the resulting disclosures provide answers to the question of whether or not the organization is performing in a sustainable manner. Moreover, they do so for each and every capital the organization can identify as vital to either itself or its stakeholders. In the MultiCapital Scorecard, therefore, sustainability acts as an organizing principle for integrated reporting. It brings together dissimilar performances into a single coordinating framework using the concept of impacts on the carrying capacities of capitals as the linchpin. That allows leaders and other users to compare progression toward sustainable levels of impact and plan to improve performance as a result. We have found no other methodology recommended by the IIRC or others that so comprehensively integrates performance measurements across impacts on diverse capitals. Yet multiple capital accounting is the core theory of performance that ought to be at the heart of contemporary reporting from now on.

Because the MultiCapital Scorecard asks "the sustainability question," it incorporates nonfinancial performance into integrated reporting alongside financial reporting and all other forms of performance reporting that leaders and stakeholders need. Indeed, financial reporting, too, in the MultiCapital Scorecard is measured and reported against sustainability standards, just as it should be.

We find it ironic that sustainability can be thought to be achievable without considering economic sustainability. To become sustainable, an organization must be economically sustainable. This applies not only to businesses, but also to organizations of all sorts. How meaningful can it therefore be to exclude economic performance from so-called sustainability performance?

Similarly, how meaningful can it be to have integrated reporting that touches on all six capitals identified by the IIRC, but fails to identify the fact that they may be operating in an entirely unsustainable manner? The

MultiCapital Scorecard reveals the gaps between sustainability standards and actual performance; <IR> does not.

We do recognize that many organizations will be reluctant to acknowledge that they are performing unsustainably. But we argue that it is better to ask the right question and deal with the gaps that appear than to ignore the question and paper over them in the performance measurement system.

The IIRC's <IR> Framework makes a sound case for multicapitalism, but implementing the <IR> Framework requires the MultiCapital Scorecard (or a similar methodology) because the <IR> Framework:

- Lacks common principles to apply to all capital impacts
- Fails to require any performance norms
- Ignores context as a vital element of capital creation measurement
- Disregards sustainability as an essential component of meaningful integrated reporting

We have consciously developed the MultiCapital Scorecard as a process that can be applied to organizations of all sorts. IIRC has chosen to focus on quoted companies because its principal audience is the financial investor and its prime concern is the stability of financial markets. It comes as no surprise, therefore, that we propose different standards and address divergent concerns.

Nevertheless, we remain firmly convinced that the MultiCapital Scorecard is the best tool available as of 2016 to operationalize the <IR> Framework. In truth, it goes well beyond the performance measurement requirements of <IR>. And as it does, it offers the most comparable analytical principles and processes for delivering the narrative requirements that IIRC specifies. The standard-setting processes of the MultiCapital Scorecard are forward looking and therefore support the forward looking statements that <IR> requires. Furthermore, the MultiCapital Scorecard's consolidation protocols allow meaningful aggregation of context-based performance at all levels: subsidiary, division, and consolidated group. It thereby lends itself to adoption by organizations of all shapes and sizes, from sole traders to multinationals.

One Report:
Integrated Reporting for a Sustainable Strategy

The book *One Report* by Eccles and Krzus was a prime mover in arguing the case for <IR> to support organizations seeking to reduce their unsustainability. Its authors, a Harvard academic and a practitioner, address executives, shareholders, and all other stakeholders. "One report" is shorthand for an integrated approach to reporting financial, social, and environmental impacts of organizational performance. The single report does not have to be a printed document. Indeed, it is most likely that users of integrated reports will increasingly tend to obtain their information via direct access to data made available by each organization to its various stakeholders. The book discusses the state of financial and nonfinancial reporting, concluding with the expectation that "stakeholders will be increasingly demanding of high-quality nonfinancial information that determines future financial results."[10] (Note that this presumes, if not imposes, the acceptance of financial primacy by subordinating nonfinancial performance to its eventual impact on financials.)

Arguments in favor of integrated reporting include:[11]

- Greater clarity about relationships between financial and nonfinancial data
- Better decisions based on better information and better internal collaboration
- Deeper engagement with all stakeholders to foster mutual respect between them
- Lower reputational risk through addressing changing expectations explicitly

Underlying all these benefits, say the authors, is the need for dialogue and engagement across the organization.

Arguments against integrated reporting cited in the book (and their refutations as shown in parentheses) are summarized as follows:[12]

- Markets are efficient and need no more nonfinancial data (but analysts forever seek more).

- Optimally managed businesses need no more information than they have (ill-advised complacency).
- *One Report* damages shareholder value-creation (incorrectly assumes a zero-sum game for others).
- There is a high cost in preparing integrated reports (but that cost is thought to be more than outweighed by the benefits of communication across the divisional silos: collaborative dialogue.)

Examples of leading integrated reporting companies show that the time lapse from committing to the concept to becoming reference organizations can easily be a decade. As users develop more direct ways of accessing integrated reporting databases, organizations that have learned how to release relevant information of a financial and nonfinancial nature in timely and complementary ways will have major competitive advantages.

For our part, we argue that value can be created or destroyed in any of the capitals: natural, human, social and relationship, economic, and constructed. None should be predispositionally subordinated to any other without considering their context. We would add that dialogue and engagement need to extend beyond the boundaries of the organization to include all stakeholder groups. *One Report* fails to make the case that "sustainability context" be the basis of normative performance standards in these ways.

Nevertheless, with these provisos, we believe that *One Report* has made a very helpful case for integrated reporting.

The MultiCapital Scorecard in Relation to *One Report*

The MultiCapital Scorecard aligns itself with the principles put forward in *One Report* and offers a genuinely integrative performance measurement process. All areas of impact are subjected to the establishment of sustainability norms applying the same principles of sustainable sufficiency: "How much is enough for the organization to be sustainable?"

And for those areas of impact in which sustainability is not within immediate reach, the question arises: What feasible trajectory would take us there soonest? That then forms the basis for measuring progression toward sustainable performance.

Because these performance measurements are all based on the same principles, and because they adopt the metrics most suited to each area of impact (for example, greenhouse gas emissions) they allow performances to be reported in meaningful terms without resorting to inappropriate monetization of all impacts. This allows the concept of a single report to be applied in a meaningful way to organizations of all sorts. Readers of an online or printed report can at a glance see in which areas of impact the organization is performing sustainably, in which it is on target to sustainable performance, in which it is just improving, and where it is making no improvement at all.

This allows management to address the areas of deficit and the areas of excess to decide how best to manage its sustainability performance facing the competing demands on resources and perhaps conflicting priorities.

UNEP

In Berlin, in November 2015, UNEP released a report in which it explicitly called for adherence to the sustainability context principle in corporate environmental reporting: *Raising the Bar—Advancing Environmental Disclosure in Sustainability Reporting*. In a section of the report titled "The Need for Context," UNEP makes the following declaration:

> *All companies should apply a context-based approach to sustainability reporting, allocating their fair share impacts on common capital resources within the thresholds of their carrying capacities.*[13]

It then adds:

> *Reporting standards/guidance bodies such as GRI, IIRC, SASB, CDP, etc. should integrate Sustainability Context more explicitly into their frameworks, for example by applying the concept of carrying capacities to multiple capitals-based frameworks.*[14]

The report also acknowledges the efforts of the Sustainability Context Group in its campaign to strengthen corporate sustainability reporting through more rigorous adherence to the sustainability context principle, and it applauds the efforts made to get GRI, IIRC, and other standards bodies to enforce it through better guidance. To have the UNEP embrace these ideas and endorse the concept is a major win for those who believe context to be essential. The MultiCapital Scorecard, too, thereby receives an endorsement for its underlying principles from one of the highest global authorities: a prime stakeholder for natural capital.

The Integrated Reporting Movement

Following on their seminal work in *One Report*, Eccles and Krzus conducted a wide-ranging and well-researched review of the whole field of integrated reporting. The later book maintains all the arguments of *One Report*, with one exception: Instead of the original assertion that "companies as the reporting entities must take the lead with the support of their boards and auditors . . . we will argue . . . that the ultimate responsibility for integrated reporting lies with the board of directors, with support from executive management and the company's auditors."[15]

The book opens with a chapter dedicated to the early development and implementation of integrated reporting in South Africa. It credits Mervyn King with the dedicated leadership of the initiative, situating it in its sociopolitical and economic context. The turbulent fields of the country as it emerged from apartheid and minority white rule demanded new governance mechanisms. Integrated reporting of social, economic, and environmental impacts offered a solution for the important corporate sector. New values of mutual respect could be fostered. Meeting the needs of the whole community could become organizational objectives. Integrated reporting facilitated the articulation of emerging ethical codes. Integrated reporting led to "integrated thinking."[16]

Integrated reporting not only helped rehabilitate the country's national image, it attracted foreign capital investment. The irony that such a globally leading governance mechanism should be adopted by the private sector in a country in which the public sector is in desperate need of something similar is diplomatically sidestepped by the authors. Although, to be fair, they do point out that the Integrated Reporting Council of South Africa (IRC of SA) addresses any organization, not just the private sector.

However, Eccles and Krzus do not sidestep another elephant-in-the-room issue. They point out that the IRC of SA code adopted by South Africa (in advance of the IIRC's 2013 <IR> Framework) addresses sustainability as "core to the discussion."[17] Indeed, in a discussion paper issued by the IRC in 2011, the authors of that paper mentioned sustainability fifty-two times. By way of "stark contrast," the <IR> Framework subsequently released in 2013 mentions sustainability only three times. The IIRC's <IR> Framework treats sustainability as "core to the discussion to the extent that it has material influence on value creation over time" and no more.[18]

Moreover, they define their audiences differently. As Eccles and Krzus put it, "The IIRC focused on 'providers of financial capital'; the IRC of SA has a multi-stakeholder approach, stating that an integrated report 'allows stakeholders to assess the ability of the organization to create and sustain value.'"[19] They point out these factual differences without delving into the underlying values that drive them. *Six Capitals*, by Jane Gleeson-White, touches on them as we note below. Clearly, there are different interpretations of value being applied here.

The Integrated Reporting Movement: Meaning, Momentum, Motives, and Materiality addresses materiality in a comprehensive manner, comparing the stance taken by regulatory bodies, AccountAbility, Carbon Disclosure Project, GRI, IIRC, and SASB.[20] Noteworthy highlights include:

- Only GRI and IIRC consider that the reporting boundary may be broader than the company (or other entity that may be the unit of analysis).
- Only GRI and AccountAbility set stakeholders as the primary intended users.

The 2015 Eccles and Krzus book remains silent on the subject of "sustainability context" in integrated reporting. Whereas GRI and others have for many years espoused the importance of such context in considering organizational performance, one of us (McElroy with Van Engelen) has been the only authority on the subject to publish a methodology for how to do it in practice. Context-Based Sustainability measurement and reporting was the essence of their 2012 book. It also lies at the heart of the MultiCapital Scorecard.

Since 2013, the Sustainability Context Group has encouraged the adoption of context-based norms into performance measurement standards. It is therefore a disappointment to see the subject almost entirely overlooked by Eccles and Krzus again in 2015. However, they do state that "what is material for a firm is entity-specific and must be determined by that firm and ratified by its board of directors."[21] This is an indirect call for sustainability context to be incorporated into all performance standards, the very essence of the MultiCapital Scorecard.

The MultiCapital Scorecard
in Relation to *The Integrated Reporting Movement*

In ways that are consistent with and complement Eccles and Krzus, the MultiCapital Scorecard contributes to integrated reporting as follows:

- It addresses all stakeholders in the same way using common principles.
- It incorporates standards that set performance norms for all impacts.
- It adopts sustainability criteria as the unifying norm across all capitals.
- It offers progression reporting as the means to achieving sustainable performance.
- It is meaningful at decentralized as well as aggregated levels of analysis.
- It adopts materiality considerations fit for all stakeholders in their own contexts.

The MultiCapital Scorecard does not provide the narrative required of the <IR> Framework's business models, but it does contribute to their development and continuing refinement with a quantified approach to setting standards and measuring actual performance. It also structures an approach to stakeholder engagement. Critically, only the MultiCapital Scorecard asks reporting entities to answer the sufficiency question: "How much is enough to be sustainable?"

Six Capitals, or Can Accountants Save the Planet?

While the Eccles and Krzus book gives a broad review of the integrated reporting movement today, Gleeson-White's book offers a longitudinal view of how today's situation emerged over millennia. But fret not! By page 22, she has covered the period from 7000 BCE with farming in Mesopotamia to 3300 BCE when "the ancient accountants . . . [created] the world's first clay tablets . . . the basis of a single-entry accounting system."[22] Then, via Luca Pacioli's 1494 *Summa de Arithmetica, Geometria, Proportione et Proportionalità*, double-entry bookkeeping and the notion of capital have been explained.[23] And by page 30, she has introduced the concept of nonfinancial value. All this is a fascinating summary of her previous book: *Double Entry—How the Merchants of Venice Created Modern Finance*.[24]

But *Six Capitals* also gives us a very readable story of how and why integrated reporting emerged, both at the micro economic level of the business and at the macro level of the state (national accounts including natural capital). It takes the thinking process beyond conventional integrated reporting and ends with an appropriately forward look, asking: "Can we save the planet?"

Commenting on the process leading up to the IIRC's publication of its <IR> Framework in December 2013, Gleeson-White reports that "for Druckman (CEO of the International Integrated Reporting Council) it is important that integrated reporting is led by the market, because if it cannot make a case for itself so that businesses want to adopt it and investors want to use it, then there is no point to it."[25]

This suggests that the CEO of IIRC believes that markets themselves cannot harbor the imperfections that may be preventing the adoption of sustainable practices. The book concludes that "the published framework makes clear that returns on financial capital have primacy over the other capitals."[26] The book goes on to discuss human capital and natural capital and whether integrated reporting and markets can achieve more efficient resource allocations:

Is allocating the world's scarce supplies of water and stocks of arable land
to grow sugarcane and beet to create sugared drinks that may contribute

160

to the rising incidence of obesity and diabetes the best use of these limited resources (water and arable land)? To me the fact that integrated reporting cannot address such questions suggests . . . [that] its promise to foster efficient resource allocations pertains only to financial capital and not to other capitals.[27]

It may well be that Gleeson-White is asking too much from integrated reporting and markets. But what is clearly true is that the resolution of the resource allocation and multiple capital reporting challenges cannot be a quick fix. The common ground of agreement between all commentators is that we all need to embark on a learning process of exploring the implications of what integrated reporting and sustainability really mean to each organization in its own context. It may thereby prove easier to act our ways into new thinking than to think our ways into new ways of acting. Gleeson-White argues that we need to intervene at the apex of Donella Meadows' hierarchy: We need to change our values.[28] Emery and Trist made this a requirement for dealing with turbulent fields in 1965.[29] Resource shortages and climate change will tend to make turbulence a continuing condition, rather than a passing storm. Commenting on Christopher Stone's related 1972 article, "Should Trees Have Standing?", Gleeson-White writes:[30]

We have created a world predicated on endless growth, because financial capital appears capable of endless growth. But we now realize that as it grows, it chews up the planet and the people it purports to serve . . . the aims of ensuring our well-being and that of nature are so mutually supportive that it is hard to see whether the reason for doing so is to advance ourselves or, as he put it, to advance a "new 'us' that includes the environment."

The MultiCapital Scorecard in Relation to *Six Capitals*

Contrary to Gleeson-White's perception of the IIRC's favoring of financial capital, the MultiCapital Scorecard goes to great lengths to ensure that no single capital has dominance over any other as a matter of principle. It does, however, offer the facility for users to weight capital impacts differently according to the perceptions and priorities of the reporting organization.

We also argue that the MultiCapital Scorecard is unrivaled in its value as a learning framework. That is not to undermine its validity as a performance measurement process. It is simply to recognize that such learning takes years and the double-loop learning process incorporated into the MultiCapital Scorecard is designed to facilitate continuous improvement. But much more important than this generic learning technique, the MultiCapital Scorecard is the only process we know that requires users to seek out for themselves what sustainable performance means to them in their own real world contexts. Moreover, this is not a handy bolt-on extra—this search lies at the very heart of the MultiCapital Scorecard. It is essential in establishing sustainability norms. This requires action learning on the ground and in situ. Better still, it involves building active links with stakeholders and listening to their own changing realities, their needs, and their aspirations.

None of this is to say that stakeholders' expressed wishes will all be granted; they obviously cannot all be granted, since many will be in conflict with the aspirations of other stakeholder groups. But as a learning mechanism, it is vital (and more so in turbulent times) to build active information flows with the vital stakeholders of the organization. Context is crucial.

Unlike the IIRC's <IR> requirements, the MultiCapital Scorecard adopts sustainability performance as the integrating concept across all capitals. It is not therefore sufficient to simply describe *that* various capitals are impacted. In setting standards to indicate what the *extent* of such impact should be, the criterion of sustainability plays a vital role in the MultiCapital Scorecard.

We accept that markets are important in many facets of resource allocation. But, like Gleeson-White, we do not believe that the new paradigms and new values required for a sustainable world have to be endorsed by current financial investors or their advisors. Indeed, it may well be that in the knowledge economy the critical investors will become those innovators and experts on whose intellectual capital the future depends. When the dinosaurs of old-world financial primacy find that they can no longer attract the talent they require, they may discover that their epoch is over. The market will indeed carry out capital allocation, but it will not be the financial market. It will be the talent market. Talented individuals will seek organizations whose own values are transparent and who favor balance and sustainability over "profit-maximization at all costs." The MultiCapital Scorecard can foster such values changes, but it takes time. There is no magic switch to turn on once the dinosaur feels the death pangs creeping up. The "Valuing your Talent" initiative in the United Kingdom will perhaps show the way, and it may adopt the MultiCapital Scorecard as its overall organizational performance framework.[31]

Shortfalls and Surpluses

Given that the MultiCapital Scorecard establishes thresholds of sustainable performance as sustainability norms, it follows that all performances meeting the threshold are sustainable. Performances that more than conform to the sustainability norm may represent capital creation (for example, additional intellectual property or more equity capital) or they may represent a usage of resources that is simply within sustainable limits. Surpluses may also indicate a wasteful use of resources. For example, spending time and money on improving the performance in an area that is already sustainable is unlikely to improve its sustainability. The MultiCapital Scorecard does not award bonus points for going beyond sustainability norms.

Indeed, the MultiCapital Scorecard makes no value judgments at all about performances that exceed the sustainability norm. Still, it may be vital to the prosperity of many organizations that they create value beyond the sustainability norm level if they are to prosper. The MultiCapital Scorecard simply highlights actual performance compared to the relevant sustainability norm. Judgments about what action to take are left to the management of the organization in its own context.

By way of contrast, all performances that fail to meet their respective sustainability norms are unsustainable. Shortfalls against standards therefore represent capital erosion, destruction, or the failure to produce it at required levels. Even if performances are improving on the past, so long as impacts fall short of the sustainability norms, they diminish or fail to maintain the carrying capacities of the vital capitals involved.

Consequently, when setting strategic goals, organizations should be aware of the areas of impact in which they are unsustainable (showing shortfalls) and those in which they are in surplus, with a view to allocating resources to meet their long-term ambitions most effectively.

In the worked examples section of this book (part 2), we illustrate the MultiCapital Scorecard for the hypothetical ABC company. Readers can follow therein our discussion of how the individual scores are calculated and how the surpluses or shortfalls occur. Thereafter, the MultiCapital Scorecards for 2015 to 2019 show the annual reports that would have been presented to the board of directors in order to shape their action plans for the coming years.

Only the MultiCapital Scorecard presents such information on a single page (or screen) using a single set of principles to allow boards to approve management's proposals on where to dedicate resources to overcome the gaps in current performance.

We also do not accept that surpluses in some areas can "compensate" in some way for deficiencies in meeting duties of care in others. The MultiCapital Scorecard does not compensate "apples with oranges." But it does aggregate progression scores. Such aggregation does not in any way compensate for unsustainable performance or misappropriate any surpluses. However, where people, time, and money are all in short supply, top management and those responsible for governance need to decide on priorities. The MultiCapital Scorecard provides a framework to allow them to do so with consistent data that is meaningful in aggregate and to the lowest level of disaggregation, too.

Double-Loop Learning

The MultiCapital Scorecard allows organizations to set relevant performance standards and requires that they learn from applying them in practice. Consequently, it is critically important to the process that it does not get stuck in its operational cycle, but takes a detached view of the whole process from time to time (see figures 9.1 and 9.2). In the operational cycle, the organization basically asks itself: "How do we close the gaps between actual performance and sustainability norms?"

However, the policy cycle needs to take into account the experience, especially the unforeseen consequences, of operating the MultiCapital Scorecard in practice in the organization's own specific context. Thus, the policy cycle asks questions that are more open-ended:

- Is our governance structure appropriate to our needs?
- Are we becoming less unsustainable?
- Have we captured all stakeholders and vital capitals in our areas of impact?
- Can we learn anything from peer group organizations?
- What do our stakeholders tell us about the way we measure performance?
- Can external assurance reports offer scope for improvement?
- Do we need to adjust our standards of performance?
- Is there a better way of working than using the MultiCapital Scorecard?

These double-loop questions may require a reappraisal of the assumptions made about the organization, its assumed context, and all other possible avenues of inquiry. To do this, everything must be open to discussion and challengeable. There can be no secrets to cover up inherent deficiencies or wrong assumptions. The characteristic of this double-loop learning is that it reexamines the governing variables: the parameters within which the operational cycle functions.

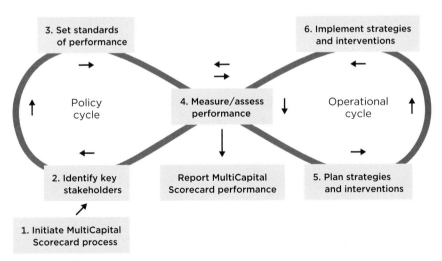

Figure 9.1. Double-loop learning cycles. In the policy cycle, standards of performance (sustainability norms and trajectory targets) are defined; in the operational cycle, performance is measured, managed, and reported against them. Adapted from McElroy and Van Engelen (2012).

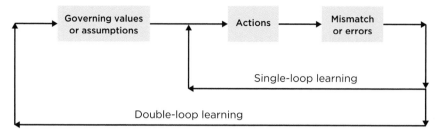

Figure 9.2. Single- and double-loop learning. Whereas single-loop learning consists of knowledge in use (sensing and responding to events based on existing knowledge), double-loop learning consists of knowledge production, especially in cases where knowledge or theories in use lead to unexpected or erroneous outcomes. Adapted from Argyris (1990).

To quote the late Chris Argyris, professor emeritus at Harvard Business School:

> *The action theory-in-use helps—indeed requires—mistaken assumptions to be reformulated, incongruities reconciled, incompatibilities resolved, vagueness specified, untestable notions made testable, scattered information brought together into meaningful patterns and previously withheld information shared.*[32]

This is, therefore, not an exercise that can be undertaken every year in most organizations. But, depending on the context of the organization, it should be conducted in depth at least every five years. Argyris continues:

> *I am also proposing that these changes become part of all long-range change programs. . . . The individuals automatically become agents for change. . . . Indeed, it should not be possible to make an informational double-loop cultural change without individuals learning new theories-in-use and new social virtues.*[33]

The importance of the double-loop policy review can therefore hardly be overstated. It distinguishes a serious learning system from a dogmatic, target-driven, top-down, hierarchical, task-oriented organization. In the terms of Larry Hirschhorn's sociopsychodynamic framework (appendix C), these policy reviews open an authorized link between the inhibited structure (the "worry gut" in which thoughts cannot become actions and so tend to produce anxiety) and the developmental structure in which the uncertainty surrounding them may be dealt with. That opens a space for dialogue and explicitly allows concerns to be articulated. Nothing is therefore undiscussable.

The developmental structure proposes new rules and new tasks to alter the "normal" authorized way of working. Some such proposals will be adopted and become the new "normal." Others will be held in the inhibiting structure. Yet others will return to the developmental structure for reformulation or reconsideration. In any case, future policy reviews will provide space for their reconsideration if that has not occurred naturally in the meantime.

One practical consideration of such periodic reviews is that they provide the place and time to approve new rules of the game across the whole spectrum of the MultiCapital Scorecard and its applications. As a result, any proposed changes to the weightings accorded to various areas of impact and any changes to or clarifications of the scoring schema can all be considered together and introduced from the same date. This should normally be the start of the next planning cycle. In this way plans already adopt the new data definitions against which actual performance will be reported after the end of the reporting period. (As a reporting protocol, it will be normal practice to express at least the past year's performance using approximations to the new definitions in order to allow comparability across the years.)

The double-loop reviews thereby provide the periodic opportunities for administrative and definitional change. This in its turn gives stability to the data definitions applicable in between reviews. Boundaries, sustainability norms, trajectory targets, areas of impact, metrics, and other data definitions should all remain constant until the next review is conducted. If not, there will be a natural tendency to change them as the need arises without widespread explanations or authorization. Reports would then suffer in both their meaning and in the integrity of the process.

External Assurance

The MultiCapital Scorecard is both a management information and performance accounting system. External assurance should therefore be undertaken with a view to the added value that the assurer can offer to management. As integrated reporting is still embryonic in most of the world as of 2016, the expertise in assuring social and environmental impacts is not well developed. However, in South Africa, where the Johannesburg stock exchange has made integrated reporting mandatory (on a comply or explain basis) since 2012 for quoted companies, specialized assurance has developed rapidly. As a leading example, IRAS (a consultancy for integrated reporting and assurance services in South Africa) has developed a deep and broad database of best practice from some two hundred leading organizations.[34] IRAS has also standardized and detailed areas of impact across a wide range of vital capitals. This wealth of information can be consulted for a modest fee.

Moreover, the assurance offered by IRAS and others can guide organizations of all sorts on the best peer group practices, including data sources and metrics adopted. Such external data provides important food for thought when management and governors set up a MultiCapital Scorecard or when they enter the double-loop reviews of their MultiCapital Scorecard processes and outcomes. External eyes offer valuable independent perspectives.

The World Business Council for Sustainable Development in its 2015 publication *Reporting Matters* offers the following assessment of current audit practice among leading businesses that have committed to sustainable development:

- *The most effective reporters publish an assurance statement that is easily accessible and provides details on the objective and scope of the assurance, including boundaries and the applied standard or regulation.*
- *The majority of assurance statements indicate the level of assurance attained (limited or reasonable).*
- *Some companies use assurance when it is required by law (GHG emissions) but do not extend it to other material issues.*
- *Very few companies indicate why and how assurance findings are subsequently used within the company.*[35]

The report goes on to specify that good practice requires companies to

engage an independent external assurance provider to a reasonable level for the most material issues and to a limited level for all other material issues, or an external verification provider on all material data and underlying reporting processes.[36]

To encourage the maximum value added by these processes, organizations should foster an open information culture in which assumptions are documented, data is retained, and decisions are logged. Similarly, the reports of assurers should be published and retained with follow-up processes documented and action plans timed and resourced for future reference.

Once the MultiCapital Scorecard becomes embedded sufficiently to be a framework for external reporting to other stakeholders, external assurance has an additional role to play: namely, assuring the quality of data, conclusions, and views expressed to stakeholders.

The MultiCapital Scorecard provides assurers with a solid support framework for several reasons:

- The theoretical underpinning of the MultiCapital Scorecard has unrivaled conceptual integrity; to our knowledge, no other sustainability performance measurement process enjoys such a theoretical framework.
- The same principles are applied to all forms of capital and the organization's impacts on them.
- The MultiCapital Scorecard asks the specific questions: "How much is enough to be sustainable, and are we?" Most other sustainability reporting processes avoid such questions and are content, instead, to simply list eco-efficiencies or allegedly good deeds.
- The metrics adopted can be the measurements best suited to the specific capital impacts in the context of the individual organization. There is consequently no need to justify the unit prices that would be needed to monetize each impact in an attempt to express all impacts in terms of pecuniary value.
- The standard setting of sustainability norms and trajectory targets can be audited in advance of reporting actual data, thereby allowing deep analysis of the scientific and ethical underpinnings of norms and peer group standards.
- As a result of all these reasons, assurers have less judgment of their own to bring to the assurance report. Data drives the conclusions. Actual performance is quantified and compared to preestablished norms.
- Laying down an adequate audit trail becomes an objective of the MultiCapital Scorecard.

The MultiCapital Scorecard therefore incorporates external assurance into a virtuous cycle. It increases management's competence and stakeholders' confidence in the processes of standard setting and reporting. Performance measurement and resource allocations to improve performance focus the efforts of management and other employees to eliminate unsustainable practices. Stakeholders can see the results of those endeavors and can contribute to improving processes, standards, and performance in constructive dialogue based on relevant information. Assurers and users can build databases of metrics and norms.

Assurers can never guarantee that all the information used is 100 percent accurate and objective, nor should stakeholders ever expect this to be the case. We reject the notion that valid concepts should be ignored if the data they produce cannot be independently assured with very high levels of confidence. We argue that it is better to be approximately right than precisely wrong. Disregarding context, disregarding sustainability, and disregarding standards of performance are all very wrong, in our view, because the absence of any one (and particularly all three) undermines the ability of users to take meaningful action on the basis of the reported information.

Assurers will draw on the growing waves of Big Data to corroborate performance across a wide range of impacts once they are required to do so. The MultiCapital Scorecard helps organizations to frame those requirements. We all do future generations an immense disservice if we fail to specify the data we need to act responsibly today.

In the end, responsibility for performance rests with management and those charged with governance. External assurance of the data they draw on helps them all, as well as providing confidence to users of the reports they produce. It also seeds the perpetual learning cycle.

CHAPTER TEN

Conclusions:
Mind the Gaps[1]

In this book we have taken a long walk through the principles and practices that we have developed for the MultiCapital Scorecard. As reflective practitioners, we are firmly of the belief that the space that needs filling lies between academe and practice. On the one hand, the deep research of multiple disciplines that characterizes the academic schools of thought is taking great strides in developing performance measurement in social and environmental accounting, while still exploring more complete concepts and processes in financial accounting. But on the other hand, little practical advice emanates from academe to guide practitioners to implement the ideas in practice.

As a consequence, practitioners and thought leaders who recognize the need to act responsibly toward social, environmental, and economic stakeholders find themselves without guidance. There is not even a cohesive set of principles on which to base their strategies or performance measurements. The turbulent times that characterize the global economic, social, and environmental conditions in which their organizations operate create changes that require new ways of working. And they have to be adopted more rapidly than ever before. Practitioners simply do not have the time to read academic literature to glean the best thinking on sustainability measurement, management, and reporting.

Accounting bodies are themselves struggling to cope with the demands of the globalizing society and the failures of market mechanisms. Meanwhile they face increasing demands for frameworks to structure the plethora of new information that information technologies are generating.

In the meantime, Earth's resources are being run down beyond the world's ability to regenerate or absorb the effluent that humankind is producing. These factors ensure that turbulence will continue into the future.

Here, therefore, we have attempted to summarize how we believe the MultiCapital Scorecard addresses these gaps, how it works, and why we think it offers a learning process and solution to help organizations of all sorts to produce meaningful integrated thinking. The best of academe and practice come together in the MultiCapital Scorecard to enable organizations to rethink what they really ought to be doing.

In addressing this issue, we have focused on gaps between:

- Knowing and doing
- Perfection and pragmatism
- Multicapitalism and financial primacy
- Standardization and meaningful standard-setting
- Top-down and bottom-up action

Context-Based Sustainability addresses these gaps for nonfinancial impacts by providing a principles-based process that organizations can use to establish sustainability performance norms applicable to their own contexts.[2] Context-Based Sustainability adopts rigorous academic standards of capital theory, Popperian fallibilism, and Rawlsian justice, while incorporating the ideas of leading scholars in sustainability to form the framework of its principles.[3] These principles allow organizations to learn from stakeholders about the performance duties and obligations they believe the organization owes them. The MultiCapital Scorecard, in turn, extends these principles and processes to include financial stakeholders, thereby completing the triple bottom line.

Conclusions: Mind the Gaps

The MultiCapital Scorecard's open-source philosophy ensures that no commercial barriers prevent the academic thinking from becoming action in practice. The MultiCapital Scorecard thereby provides a practical process for practitioners to engage with academe and address regulatory requirements as well.

One joy of context-based norming is that it produces intensely relevant learning that makes real meaning without standardizing concepts or metrics into a one-size-fits-all form. This bridges the second gap: users set the best standards possible, not awaiting perfect solutions. This starts learning from doing. Moreover, the MultiCapital Scorecard tests and argues for impact standards that would be applicable if all other entities adopted the same principles, very much along the lines of Kant's "categorical imperative."[4] It does not therefore need to wait for a fully sustainable environment to be created.

The MultiCapital Scorecard recommends engaging all members of the organization who wish to participate. Leadership and decision making can come from the top of the hierarchy, but stakeholder engagement and the search for sustainability norms should be bottom-up. Self-renewal should be driven from every seat in the organization.[5] Engaging younger generations in change processes allows new values to feed into more progressive outcomes.[6] A second joy of the MultiCapital Scorecard is that it lends itself to such bottom-up work. Sustainability norms are socially constructed, just as they should be.

Genuine multicapitalism accords no primacy to any particular stakeholder group. Consequently, the MultiCapital Scorecard's multicapital materiality perspective introduces a materiality matrix that is entirely new. It avoids the doctrinaire monetization of nonfinancial impacts, which characterizes the <IR> solutions offered by leading accounting firms. Instead, the MultiCapital Scorecard sets sustainability standards of performance in the most meaningful way by direct reference to an organization's own contextually relevant, capital-specific units of measurement, be they monetary or otherwise. Indeed, whereas many academic sustainability analyses prefer to avoid monetization, we have so far come across no practical solution for how to do so other than the MultiCapital Scorecard.

A Broad View of How the MultiCapital Scorecard Works

In broad strokes, the MultiCapital Scorecard methodology generally follows a three-step pattern of activity as follows:

1. Scoping and materiality
2. Areas of impact (AOIs) development
3. Scorecard implementation

Scoping and Materiality

The first step in applying the MultiCapital Scorecard is scoping and materiality. It consists of the following major activities:

Boundaries of the entity to be assessed are defined. This may include boundaries that extend beyond the financial boundaries of the reporting unit itself; how else could it deal with shared capital and externalities? It is also vital to identify early on whether the reporting entity is to be broken down into subdivisions, or conversely consolidated with others into group totals.

Vital capitals and relevant stakeholders are considered. Identifying the relevant capitals and stakeholders whose well-being depends on them can be an iterative process, but is an essential starting point.

The materialities of AOIs are then assessed. The MultiCapital Scorecard has a protocol to determine absolute materiality. The process then proceeds to accord weights, sizes, and progression scores to each AOI, providing a relative materiality to each, encapsulating qualitative materiality in novel form.

Areas of Impact (AOIs) Development

Once a material set of AOIs has been identified for an organization, each of the associated AOIs must be further researched and developed in preparation

174

for the role it will play in measurement, management, and reporting. This consists of the following activities:

The specification of sustainability norms: We define sustainability norms as standards of performance for what an organization's impacts on vital capitals must be in order to be sufficient, sustainable, and supportive of stakeholder well-being. A sustainability norm for water use might say what an organization's consumption of water should be in volumetric terms (for example, a not-to-exceed level in liters, determined by reference to some measure of entitlement).

The specification of trajectory targets: Sometimes, the sustainability norms identified for particular AOIs will not be achievable all at once, in which case the MultiCapital Scorecard allows for the specification of trajectory targets as interim goals.

The specification of data collection protocols: Once sustainability norms and trajectory targets have been defined for individual AOIs, data collection protocols for each must be developed in order to acquire information for purposes of populating a MultiCapital Scorecard. The dimensions of such protocols will typically be people, processes, and technologies.

Scorecard Implementation

The MultiCapital Scorecard is a concise, single-screen report that shows the periodic performance of all components (AOIs) of the triple bottom line. It compares actual impacts on vital capitals to organization-specific sustainability standards of performance. Once the first and second steps above have been completed, the formatting of data into the MultiCapital Scorecard is a simple task. But the simplicity of design is essential to providing governors of organizations an overview of progression. It should not be mistaken for oversimplification. The scorecard allows managers and directors:

- To see at a glance which AOIs (and bottom line scores) show a sustainable performance. This is indicated by those impacts scoring 100 percent (actual performances versus their corresponding sustainability norms).

175

- To see at a glance which AOIs and bottom lines fall short of 100 percent. In their cases, the MultiCapital Scorecard indicates progression toward sustainability norms. Of course, progression is never linear, but the MultiCapital Scorecard's seven-point progression scale offers approximations ranging from +100 percent (for full sustainability) to -100 percent (for multiyear regression with no plans to improve). The latter is close to "willful or reckless capital destruction." It does not mean that all capital will be destroyed. It does mean that major changes are needed to steer the organization toward a sustainable future.
- To see aggregated progression scores that offer an "overall performance" total. This is a single score that reports the triple bottom line performance of an organization. It makes no assumption of intercapital substitution, as it is a measure of progression, not of sustainability per se. However, as an annual performance indicator, it shows broadly whether an organization is moving toward or away from its sustainability norms.

As sustainability norms are the context-based sustainability standards of triple bottom line performance, we consider the whole process—including this broad total indicator—a useful management tool to guide organizations toward becoming less unsustainable.

Once organizations have internalized the need to formulate their strategies toward triple bottom line performance, they are faced with the challenge of how to make their major decisions. Clearly financial investment analysis alone will not do the job. Social and environmental factors need to be considered. Indeed, in some cases the major investment decisions will be driven by the need to accomplish nonfinancial goals.

The MultiCapital Scorecard frames such decision-making processes by already having:

- Identified the various stakeholders and vital areas of impact
- Weighted the importance of each AOI to the organization concerned
- Determined the performance standards required to become sustainable
- Established trajectory targets for their accomplishment

Thus, the MultiCapital Scorecard helps organizations to bridge the potentially fatal gap between planning and implementation. The concepts, the language, the engagement of stakeholders, the priorities, and the timetables all come together to give the triple bottom line implementation its greatest chance of success.

Other Ways the MultiCapital Scorecard Bridges the Gaps

As the MultiCapital Scorecard is a completely new development, it is not surprising that it has yet to be tested in many practical implementations. Nevertheless, its principles have been roundly endorsed by two subsidiaries of large multinational companies in which it is being piloted (Unilever and a US-based consumer products company). Both subsidiaries have been actively committed to sustainability principles for many years, and both welcomed the MultiCapital Scorecard, with one calling it "the most promising performance measurement process for integrated reporting that we have yet encountered."[7]

In this regard, it has proven important to users that the MultiCapital Scorecard exceeds the demands of the IIRC and GRI without requiring compliance with either. Interestingly, in both companies, sustainability teams led the way with the MultiCapital Scorecard. But this should not be surprising. In general, finance departments seem unaware of <IR> or other regulatory requirements that may demand integrated reporting functions. This was the experience of South Africa until "King III" introduced an "apply or explain why not" policy to quoted companies in its 2009 report.[8]

Once multinational companies mandate <IR> throughout their international organizations, we may expect to see the MultiCapital Scorecard or something like it adopted as the default mode of leading-edge sustainability reporting and integrated management.

The MultiCapital Scorecard has also been designed to suit the reporting requirements of multidivisional organizations. In particular, it allows certain AOIs to be mandated centrally, with sustainability norms and metrics also determined centrally as appropriate. So, for climate change mitigation endeavors, the center may adopt a sustainability norm of zero CO_2e emissions by 2050 for all divisions in all countries. Equally, for its return on capital employed, it may specify 10 percent after taxes as its weighted average cost of capital and set a zero residual income sustainability norm on this basis. In each of these cases, this central determination of norms and metrics allows rich data to be collected for absolute performance in the metric determined. The central data collection will then provide better performance information for central and group analysis. For all other AOIs, the organization may devolve sustainability norms target setting to local levels. Consolidation would then be scores of sustainability and progression performance only. This combination of locally and centrally determined norms supports meaningful standard-setting in the organization concerned at both local and consolidated levels. Context-based management and integrated thinking can therefore be fostered at all levels within the organization.

We recommend external assurance of the MultiCapital Scorecard and all its underlying assumptions and workings. Initially, the external assurances will be directed to managers and governors sponsoring the MultiCapital Scorecard. As integrated reporting becomes more generalized as a reporting practice, the audience for external assurance of the MultiCapital Scorecard will switch from internal only to the inclusion of external stakeholders of all sorts. We contend that the MultiCapital Scorecard facilitates more meaningful assurance than any other sustainability process we know of.

The preparatory work in the MultiCapital Scorecard allows validation of its principles and data sources in advance of reporting cycles, thereby taking much assurance work offline at peak times. Norms prepared in advance of actual performance data allow the numbers to drive conclusions, thereby reducing the scope for divergent opinions. The MultiCapital Scorecard's innovative materiality approach, too, seems to us to be similarly supportive of professional independent assurance practices.

The MultiCapital Scorecard also features a double-loop learning process that takes place periodically. We fully expect the external assurance opinions and their workings, as well as peer group comparisons conducted in the assurance process, to be constructive inputs to such double-loop reviews.

Thus, learning to improve has a process and a data source of its own within the MultiCapital Scorecard, a bridge to closing the gaps between thinking and doing. Rethinking organizational performance toward sustainable futures starts here!

APPENDIX A

Causal Textures:
Environments and Organizations

Table A.1 summarizes the key elements of the social ecology school's thinking on turbulence. Each type of causal texture is described in increasing levels of disturbance. Reading down the columns indicates the strategies, organization, and learning needed to deal with each texture. In the half century since Emery and Trist introduced the concept of *turbulent fields* (in 1965) the Western world has learned that successful strategies need to embrace the values of the society in which they operate. It has become clear that new values need to be developed to allow cohesive action in times of turbulence. The capacity to adapt to environmental challenges will set the survivors apart from the others. The table sums up the challenges that organizations face in striving for sustainability. Listening to stakeholders feeds relevant external information into the heart of the successful organization. The MultiCapital Scorecard is designed to address all these challenges in a constructive manner. Failure to deal with turbulent fields threatens deeper types of disturbed contexts. Context drives all else.

TABLE A.1. Causal Textures Environments and Organizations

TYPE	ENVIRONMENT	CHARACTERISTICS
1	Placid Randomized (Emery & Trist)	Economist's classical market. Static.
2	Placid Clustered (Emery & Trist)	Economist's imperfect competition. Stable.
3	Disturbed Reactive (Emery & Trist)	Economist's oligopolistic market. More than one big player seeking same pot of resources. Dynamic.
4	Turbulent Fields (Emery & Trist)	Not just the interaction of organizations; "The ground is in motion." Increased reliance on R&D to build learning capability. Interdependency between economic and other social spheres.
TRANSITIONAL	Hyper-Turbulent (McCann & Selsky)	Partitioned. "Enclaves" attract scarce resources. "Vortices" are left without resources or skills needed to adapt to the environment.
5	Vortical (Baburoglu)	Failure of active adaptation. Reversion to maladaptation: (1) Monothematic dogmatism (2) Stalemate (3) Polarization

Source: Martin P. Thomas, "Scenarios Towards Social Dialogue," in *Business Planning for Turbulent Times*, eds. Ramirez et al. (London: Earthscan, 2008), chap. 9.

Causal Textures

SUCCESSFUL STRATEGY	ORGANIZATIONS	LEARNING CONSEQUENCES
Tactics (= strategy) "Optimal strategy is just doing one's best on a purely local basis."	Distributed.	Optimal position is learned by trial and error.
Strategy dominates over tactics. Keys are distinctive competencies and "optimal location."	Central control and coordination grow central hierarchies.	Knowledge of the environment becomes critical to success.
"Operations" (campaigns of tactical initiatives) lie between strategy and tactics. Key is capacity to move more or less at will to make and meet competitive challenge.	Flexibility needs decentralization. Premium on quality and speed of decision at peripheral points. Interdependence emerges.	"One has to know when NOT to fight to the death." Dynamic stability is obtained by a coming to terms between competitors.
Values become "power fields" overriding both strategy and tactics. Effective emerging values create ethical codes that enable simplified action to diverging causal strands. "Institutionalization" (embodying society's values) becomes strategic objective.	Individual organizations cannot adapt alone. Collaborative relationships between dissimilar organizations. "Organizational matrix" helps to attenuate effects of turbulence. Values must be shared between all parts of the matrix for this to be effective.	(1) Increase in "relevant uncertainty." (2) Unpredictable results of actions; may not fall off with distance, but be amplified. (3) Emergent environmental forces may attenuate strong action. *Nota bene*, changes in values take about a generation to develop.
Adaptive capacity to deal with the "relevant uncertainty" is the determinant of short-term success (enclave formation). Social triage—deliberate partitioning of the field.	Field partitioned by triage policy into enclaves and vortices, with minimal interaction between them.	Decoupling of interdependencies. Dysfunctional vortex relationships threatening to affect enclaves.
Double-loop learning to develop new skills and more resources is needed for long-term removal of vortices. Collective and external strategy is needed. Maybe temporary or permanent surrender.	Apparently sealed off from the environment, but not really. Parts effectively immobilize each other.	Decline of vortices depends on external forces, as internal adaptive capacity is inadequate. Surrender may lead to reemergence.

APPENDIX B

The Sustainability Code:
A Policy Model for Achieving Sustainability in Human Social Systems
By Mark W. McElroy, PhD (2006)[1]

Introduction

Many years ago, the well-known science fiction writer Isaac Asimov wrote of futuristic societies in which intelligent robots would work in the service of humans.[2] At the most fundamental level of design, Asimov's robots were indelibly programmed with what he called the Three Laws of Robotics: (1) A robot may not injure a human being, or, through inaction, allow a human being to come to harm; (2) A robot must obey the orders given it by human beings except where such orders would conflict with the First Law; and (3) A robot must protect its own existence as long as such protection does not conflict with the First or Second Laws.

When viewed from a Knowledge Management perspective, Asimov's laws correspond to an instrumental level of behavior on the part of robots. In other words, his laws apply to the actions or potential actions of robots, to things they might do in the material world. But there is a precursor to action that Asimov's laws did not address—his laws did not address learning. In phi-losophy, we call the study of laws of learning, or innovation, epistemology.[3] Let us imagine for a moment, then, what it might mean to design robots with hard-coded epistemologies, and how their capacity to learn—as well as what they learn—might differ depending on the epistemologies we give them.

Consider two identical robots, equal in every respect except for their respective epistemologies—one with a realist epistemology and the other with a relativist epistemology. Chances are, when faced with the same set of circumstances, these two robots will develop very different conclusions about the world around them, and what actions they should each take in response. Note, as well, that all such different actions could fully comply with Asimov's Three Laws, despite the fact that their underlying epistemolo-gies and factual bases are different. The point is that Asimov's Laws are laws of action, whereas epistemologies are laws of learning.

Now let us turn to the real world of humans in modern times. We, too, are constrained by laws of action at many different levels of analysis. We are constrained by moral laws in our families and communities; by formal laws in our legal systems; and by administrative or procedural laws in our organi-zations. Our learning laws, or rules, however, are not so well defined. Still, we rely on them, utterly, for our survival, but they are not explicit. Nonetheless, they determine how we think, how we view the world, and how we reach conclusions about truth, and what should pass as knowledge for us.

Because action is nothing more than knowledge in use, the quality of our conclusions from learning matters greatly in terms of the quality of our actions, and whether or not our actions are effective, beneficial, and sustain-able. Can we not say, then, that epistemology is a variable in sustainability? I believe we can.[4] To the extent that action taken on the basis of truth is more likely to be effective, epistemology is very much a factor in the sustainability of actions and outcomes. Truth and sustainability are joined at the hip, but how to arrive at the truth is not so clear.

Indeed, when the day comes when scientists are faced with the question of how best to endow robots with a capacity to learn, which laws or rules of learning will they choose? Will the robots and electronic brains of the future be relativists or realists? Will they rely on the correspondence theory of truth or the coherence theory? Or will they be pragmatists or instrumentalists?

And if the choices scientists ultimately make on these matters have impact on the actions taken by robots and their sustainability, can we not say the same for ourselves, even now in present times?

The Sustainability Code

Last year [2005], a colleague of mine, Joseph M. Firestone, and I sat down to expressly take up the question above—not about robots, of course, but about human beings. We asked ourselves: If what people on Earth want is a pattern of action that is effective, beneficial, and sustainable, what must their learning systems be in order to meet those goals? If effective learning is the precursor to effective action, what rules, laws, or principles of learning should we have in order to maximize the quality of our learning—to achieve sustainable innovation?

We started by acknowledging that truth matters in the conduct of human affairs; that if what people want is the ability to take effective action, they should predicate their behaviors on the basis of truth, not falsity—for falsity arguably leads to ineffective action. Thus, it is always better to take action on the basis of the way the world really is. Here, we admittedly adopted a realist epistemology, a metaphysical assumption that the world in fact exists, and that we can therefore interact with it, describe it, and evaluate it.[5] Why did we take this position? Simply because we had no reason to believe otherwise.

Next in our formulation was a decision to give priority to sustainability as a desired outcome from effective learning. We called our set of rules, or laws, the Sustainability Code: "Sustainability" because we saw learning as an adaptive strategy for living systems, and "Code" because of the prescriptive or regulatory sense in which that word is sometimes used. What we were trying to create, then, was a prescriptive policy model that innovation managers could use in order to operationalize sustainable innovation, and sustainability, in human collectives.

Thus, the Sustainability Code was born. It is a policy model for organizations and other human social systems that managers can use in their attempts to cultivate sustainable innovation: a pattern of rules or requirements for organizational learning and problem solving that is more productive than mainstream approaches to innovation management, and which helps its practitioners to adapt. Thus, it is a target-state model; a target state that can be used as a "blueprint" or specification for aiding in the development of sustainable innovation, with an eye towards achieving sustainability in the conduct of human affairs.

Let us now examine the components of the Sustainability Code, a prescriptive set of eleven rules, or policies, for learning:

1. *All knowledge used as a basis for individual and/or shared action by members in a collective—in the context of the collective—shall always be open to criticism, and no such knowledge shall ever be regarded by any member as true with certainty. This is the FALLIBILITY rule.*

This rule stems from (a) the realist epistemology we chose and (b) our conviction that all human knowledge is irreparably fallible. Thus, it would be unsustainable to take action on the basis of the view that knowledge of any kind is true with certainty, since it would only serve to insulate potentially false knowledge from criticism or correction, and expose us to undue risks arising from actions predicated on mistakes.

2. *All organizational knowledge in the collective shall be accessible and transparent to all members, regardless of management roles or structures in place. No such knowledge shall be withheld from a member of the collective by any other member, except in cases where fulfilling fiduciary duties or the need to respect privacy entitlements are involved. This is the TRANSPARENCY rule.*

The principle of transparency is fundamental to effective learning, innovation, and survival. For how can we expect people to adapt to their circumstances if information about their circumstances is hidden from them? Thus, opacity, the opposite of transparency, is unsustainable as a policy for learning.

3. *All learning and innovation processes in the collective shall be accessible to, and inclusive of, all members, regardless of whatever separate*

*and/or restricted management roles or structures may be in place. This
is the INCLUSIVENESS rule.*

We sometimes refer to this concept as epistemic inclusiveness. What it
means is that stakeholders, or members of a human social system, must be
permitted to have access to, and participate in, the learning, innovation, and
knowledge processing activities of the collective. Excluding individuals from
such processes only engenders resentment, and deprives the broader population of its own members' capacity to learn and solve problems.

4. *All learning and innovation in the collective shall be rooted in the
   principle of fair critical comparison, such that prevailing or competing
   knowledge claims may always be criticized, tested, and evaluated
   against one another in a fair and complete way. This rule shall apply
   to claims of what such tests themselves should consist of, and not just
   to the primary claims to which such tests may be applied. This is the
   FAIR COMPARISON rule.*

This principle stems from the distinction between theories of truth and
theories of evaluation. Even when we have settled on theories of truth, such
as the realist theory and the correspondence method that usually accom-
panies it, we are still left with questions about how to test and evaluate
competing beliefs or claims. The Fair Comparison test is a specific theory
of evaluation; it was originally developed by Joseph M. Firestone.[6] It was
later incorporated into a theory of Knowledge Management put forward
by Firestone and McElroy, known as The New Knowledge Management.[7, 8]

5. *All members of the collective shall employ their best efforts to seek,
   recognize, and formulate problems in existing knowledge through
   critical evaluation of the performance of that knowledge in action.
   This is the LOOKING FOR TROUBLE rule.*

The purpose of learning and innovation is to help us adapt by allowing
us to close our epistemic, or knowledge, gaps. Learning is our adaptive strategy.[9] Therefore, the most adaptive human collectives will be those in which

the search for epistemic gaps is a deliberate and continuous one. Trouble, in this context, would consist of epistemic gaps that we might not be aware of, but which could be discovered if only we looked for them.

> 6. *The actual or potential performance of knowledge in action shall be defined to include the social and environmental impacts of actions taken, and in particular the sustainability of such impacts. No such impacts shall arbitrarily be externalized or otherwise excluded from the scope of evaluations performed under rule number 5 above, and all such impacts determined to be unsustainable shall be internally costed accordingly in related evaluations. This is the INTERNALIZATION rule.*

This is a terribly important rule that goes to the very heart of the sustainability crisis in the world today.[10] To the extent that businesses around the world are externalizing many of their negative social and environmental impacts, knowledge of such impacts as a precursor to related actions is also being externalized. This is a prescription for disaster in the conduct of human affairs, and it must be rejected if we are to make any progress in improving the sustainability of our course. Thus, knowledge of externalized social and environmental impacts (and their costs) must be internalized in the learning routines of a collective, as if the impacts (and costs) were internal to the collective itself. The performance measurement and reporting systems of businesses, in particular, should be structured accordingly.

> 7. *Members of the collective may produce any new rule not otherwise specified by these rules, so long as it and the learning system used to produce it do not contravene these rules. This is the GROWTH OF KNOWLEDGE rule.*

Sustainability and effective performance requires the continuous production of new knowledge in order to make adaptation possible.[11] The fact that we have established these learning-related rules is not to say that knowledge of other kinds cannot, or should not, be produced. Of course, it should.

8. *Rule numbers 1 through 7 shall apply to not only knowledge claims of fact, but also to knowledge claims of value as well. This is the FACT/ VALUE rule.*

This rule acknowledges the all-important distinction between our knowledge of facts and our knowledge of values.[12] We simply mean to suggest here that both kinds of knowledge are subject to the same principles of learning, and that sustainability in the conduct of human affairs is not just a function of our knowledge of facts, but also of our knowledge of values, too.

9. *The collective shall establish a Knowledge Management function that will be independent of the Executive Function and invested with enforceable authority to (1) allocate resources for enhancing all learning and innovation in the collective, (2) change and enhance all knowledge processing rules, (3) handle crises in knowledge processing, and (4) negotiate for resources with other organizational functions. This is the KNOWLEDGE MANAGEMENT rule.*

Rules and policies for learning and innovation require management, if only to aid in their implementation and use. This is a definition of Knowledge Management that sees itself as a management discipline that seeks to enhance the quality of learning and innovation in a social system. Moreover, it is a management discipline that a social system must have if its patterns of learning are to be sustainable, and themselves adaptive.

10. *The Knowledge Management function shall adopt and implement only knowledge processing policies that are aligned or synchronized with the self-organizing tendencies of people in organizations to produce and integrate knowledge as they will. This is the POLICY SYNCHRONI- ZATION rule.*

People have a tendency to self-organize around the discovery of problems (epistemic gaps) and the social knowledge production and integration activities that follow. A sustainable innovation system will be one that is consistent with these tendencies, and which does not either (a) conflict with or undermine them or (b) engender learning or innovation outcomes that have the effect of working against people, not for them. Indeed, a sustainable innovation system will be one that actually helps people to adapt, not maladapt!

> 11. *Any member who fails to abide by these rules shall be subject to exclusion from the collective by its other members, at their discretion. This is the ENFORCEMENT rule.*

Collective living need not amount to a suicide pact in the event that some members choose to put others at risk. To the extent that the Sustainability Code is a policy model designed to enhance the capacity of a collective to adapt, survive, and live in sustainable ways, members who work against these goals may justifiably be excluded from the community by their peers who remain committed to sustainability principles.

Conclusions

For an organization or society to be sustainable, it must have two things: knowledge of its impact on the world, and the ability to learn or innovate in response. For this reason, conscious attention must be paid to managing the epistemology of a social system, for it is the epistemology of a system that makes understanding and innovation possible. Thus, we can say that an epistemology, or innovation system, that meets these two criteria is sustainable, whereas one that does not, is not. Sustainable action requires sustainable innovation.

The concept of sustainable innovation, then, rests in part on the distinction between learning and action. In other words, we can differentiate between the sustainability of what a business, for example, produces, and the sustainability of the internal innovation processes it relies on for problem solving and learning. In general, we can say that unsustainable innovation processes will more often beget unsustainable innovations or outcomes, and that such innovation processes are more likely to work against us than for us.

It should also be clear that in many mainstream business settings, a majority of the rules set forth above are missing. While the predominant corporate epistemologies in most multinational corporations are admittedly realist in form, their learning-related policies are too often regressive. In most cases, for example, organizational knowledge is justified by appealing to the authority of management (violates Rules 1, 4, and 5 above), and most official organizational knowledge is too closely held and developed by management (violates Rules 2, 3, 7, and 10).

Of even more concern is the failure of most organizations to fully take their external social and environmental impacts into account as they make plans and assess their own performance (violates Rules 6 and 8). In the process, not only are the full factual implications of organizational operations overlooked, but so are the evaluational or value-based reactions we can have when confronted with our impacts in the world around us.

Alas, most organizations take a rather reductionist and mechanistic approach to the management of innovation, choosing to solve artificial problems with artificial processes, and thereby miss out on benefiting from the real potential of human creativity and problem solving (violates Rule 10). Instead, aberrations of our rule number 11 are enforced, according to which people are punished or excluded from a collective simply because of their desire to participate in the innovation processes of the organization.

In sum, the key question raised by this essay is: Is mainstream innovation, or even the pattern of innovation that we very often aspire to achieve, sustainable? My contention is that it is not, and that innovation pursued for its own sake, or for the sake of commerce or profit unabated, is irresponsible. Why? Because it is unsustainable, and because the price of unconstrained innovation is usually social and environmental degradation. To be sustainable, a pattern of innovation must be accompanied, stimulated, and encouraged by the kinds of policies I offer above.

The theory presented here, then, is that innovation is a variable process, and that it can either serve our purposes or defy them, depending on whether it makes it possible for us to understand our impacts in the world and adjust our actions accordingly. To the extent that it does, it can serve our purposes; but to the extent that it can distract us from such understanding, or worsen our social or environmental impacts, it can be our nemesis. The choice is up to us.

In the final analysis there are no guarantees—sustainable innovation will not necessarily lead to sustainable action. Indeed, the outcome of innovation is never predictable. Still, we can ask: Can there be sustainability in the conduct of human affairs without sustainable innovation? From the perspective of a realist epistemology, I think the answer is clearly no.

Larry Hirschhorn's Psychodynamic Framework

What the Psychodynamic Process Represents

Larry Hirschhorn, organizational behavior researcher, memorably claimed that his psychodynamic framework chart set out "all that he knew" about psychological processes (see figure C.1). Although that claim was an obvious understatement of his knowledge, the framework can help us understand the way people's thoughts are processed. This includes both conscious and unconscious thought processes. It applies to the individual and to groups of people, too. When applied to collective thinking, it is termed a sociopsychodynamic framework.

The framework adopts flow principles, using a metaphor from plumbing or electrical circuitry. Consequently, it runs the risk of oversimplification (as do all metaphors). This is a particularly pertinent consideration when attempting to explain processes of the human mind, which is perhaps the most complex system that mankind has yet discovered or invented. With this proviso, therefore, the following paragraphs attempt a simplified explanation

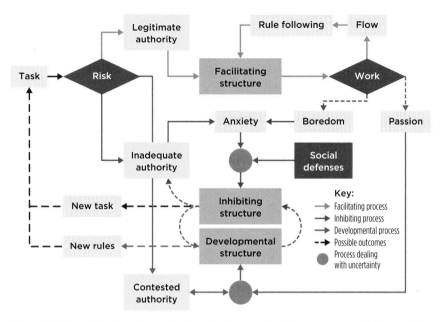

Figure C.1. Larry Hirschhorn's psychodynamic framework. Why some uncertainties result in anxiety and others in new ways of working. Diagram adapted from lecture notes and private correspondence between Martin Thomas and Larry Hirschhorn, published with Hirschhorn's permission.

of how thoughts become actions, or, perhaps more importantly, why some thoughts are prevented from becoming actions.

It is a truism that all models are wrong, but some are useful. This psychodynamic model may help groups of people understand why they can do some things easily and why other tasks simply never get done. It appears to us that this may help readers address the question of why the world takes so little action toward addressing many of the wrongs that lead us away from sustainable performance. If we understand such critical matters a little more, we may be able to enable organizations to accomplish a lot more. In such a case it will indeed prove to be a useful model, albeit an imperfect one.

How It Works

The framework contemplates three distinct but linked circuits for thought processing. They are color-coded in the framework: green, red, and blue.

Green, for "Go," represents the **facilitating structure**, in which the mind feels fully authorized and able to deal with the particular task it is given and conducts the processing as a matter of routine. The work is done by following rules that are "hard-wired" into the brain. This hard-wiring allows a flow of thought processes to enable the routine tasks to be carried out at minimal cost to the mind and without incurring the social risks implicit in operating in new (unauthorized) ways.

This flow of normal thought processes results in two possible outlets that take the tasks away from satisfactory completion. Passion for finding a better way of dealing with such matters may take the task to the developmental structure described below. Boredom resulting from doing a routine task may result in the task not reaching a satisfactory completion, resulting in its falling into the inhibiting structure, also described below.

Whereas it may be true that in many organizations the normal flow of thoughts within pre-established rules represents the bulk of the work to be done, it is never the case that it deals with 100 percent of the tasks in the minds of the people involved. Nevertheless, many change management processes and leadership initiatives in organizations of all sorts are designed as if the flow of rule following were always the case. Mechanistic changes of rules and regulations fail time after time as a result of their failure to address tasks that end up in the inhibiting structure. In other words, people are not machines: Their minds are not turned on or turned off at the flick of a switch. Change always introduces uncertainties, which threaten to become anxieties. Uncertainties challenge the authority to deal with the normal processing as if uncertainty were absent.

Red, for "Stop," indicates the **inhibiting structure**, a circuit in which tasks are prevented (unauthorized for whatever reason) from completing satisfactorily. Here is where the tasks that the unconscious (or conscious) feels to be unauthorized reside. If the uncertainties cannot be resolved, they fester into anxieties and raise social defenses to prevent the individual or group from suffering from or confronting the anxieties. Such social defenses may take one or various elements of many forms. Rejection, transference, and denial are all social defenses that may be raised by uncertainty or anxiety. They act to prevent the satisfactory processing of the task, which consequently remains in the "worry gut" of the individual or group.

Effective change management needs to address the tasks that accumulate in this holding structure. Dialogic processes can help articulate the symptoms. This is a start toward dealing with the tasks. Three routes are open, as shown in figure C.1 and explained below:

Route one. Singly or together, existing tasks stuck in the inhibiting structure may produce new tasks. New circumstances in the context or environment of the person or people may also contribute to reconsideration of previously inadequately authorized tasks. The unconscious mind is adept at creating links between disparate thoughts. Combining or reframing unauthorized tasks can allow the newly emergent tasks to be legitimately authorized and therefore to pass into the flow process of the facilitating structure. It is worth emphasizing here that the explicit engagement with others to consider and reconsider the context (iteratively if necessary) offers a positive process to help inhibited tasks to become reconfigured and thereby enter the flow of normal work.

Route two. Alternatively, the thoughts that emerge may suggest a new way of working. The outlet from the inhibiting structure would in such cases lead to the developmental structure (which we deal with below). This is no trivial matter. Indeed, new ways of working are the essence of both change management and the needs of a less unsustainable world. It is the contention of both the authors of this book that there are many people in many organizations whose thoughts on the subject of sustainable behaviors are trapped in their collective organizational inhibiting structures. As a consequence, providing people with opportunities to articulate their feelings and thoughts provides a first step toward unleashing their energies from within the organization. Freeing people and their thinking from the social defenses that shackle them in their daily lives is the key that unlocks the energy within. Moreover, sustainability cannot be accomplished by top-down instructions alone.

Route three. Lastly, we must recognize that there will always remain some tasks that are too hard to complete. The uncertainty surrounding them will turn to anxiety so long as the task remains in the process. Consequently, the last route is no escape at all; the task simply stays in the inhibiting structure.

Blue shows processes that are subject to innovation: the **developmental structure**. Innovative processes always have to deal with uncertainty. There are by definition no firm rules to follow. Moreover, the boundaries of permitted innovation are seldom clear, and the resources available to the innovative process are uncertain. But the needs for new rules and new ways of working increase as turbulence increases. Definitions of sustainable futures can be debated ad infinitum. Awaiting perfect solutions is a counsel of despair. We detect a widespread recognition of the need for more effective innovation involving people from "every seat in the organization" (to quote Gill Ringland et al. in *Beyond Crisis*).[1] This developmental structure is where thinking tasks are channeled to developing and defining new rules by which the individual or group should work.

People should know that they need not come up with perfect solutions; partial fixes or even errors are part of the learning process. The greater risk lies in denying the need for action, or expecting new ways of working to emerge from only the "traditionally authorized" facilitating structures.

Society in general, organizations in particular, and individuals everywhere need the ability to undertake the thinking and discussions needed to propose new rules, new ways of working. Leaders of organizations facing change need to think about how to make it explicit to everyone within the organization that they have a right or even a duty to contribute to developing new ways of thinking and working. This is the exact antithesis of the modern industrial Taylorist mentality of people doing all they are told and only what they are told to do in their jobs.[2]

In the postmodern era of sustainable organizations, it is incumbent on every individual to contribute to the progression of organizations toward sustainable futures. A well-defined developmental structure is an essential component of an adaptive and resilient context-based organization.

Every task entering the mental process faces the risk of rejection or failure. This is the first point of mental triage: The route of the task depends on the perceived authority of the individual or group to take that risk.

In the light of the importance of the developmental structure in actively facilitating new ways of working, we believe (and Larry Hirschhorn concurs) that the initial triage should have an exit channel of tasks entering the thought process to lead directly to the developmental structure. In other words, organizations and individuals should develop explicit authority for people to articulate their innovative thoughts and share them with others as part of their normal everyday behaviors. Development of new rules should not then need to result only from frustrated thoughts and feelings emerging from the inhibiting structure (the "worry gut") or from the supercharged passion of enthusiastic thinkers in the facilitating structure (the "day job"). Here we have another key to unlocking change from within the organization. New ideas, even crazy ideas, are okay. Welcome to renewal from within.

The Framework's Relevance to the MultiCapital Scorecard

The MultiCapital Scorecard offers organizations a toolkit to accomplish deep-rooted change through evolutionary processes. Applying the principles of capitalism to the natural and social capitals of the world alongside the economic capital (that has traditionally driven organizational growth) is a challenge in itself. But the idea that organizations should unleash powerful change from within will strike some as a step too far.

And yet, command and control will not accomplish the transition in the DNA of organizations that they will require to embrace sustainable behaviors from all their employees and contractors. Turbulent markets and turbulent societies will become ever more disturbed unless business and other organizations deal with the global resource challenges we all face. New contexts will require ever more adaptive capacity. That means new rules are needed as a matter of routine.

The MultiCapital Scorecard requires active engagement with stakeholders of all sorts in order to feed duties and obligations felt by "the context" into the norms of performance across all vital capitals. These processes cannot be confined to top management or to the "head office." Indeed, the MultiCapital Scorecard is designed specifically to be decentralized and meaningful to operators in the field and in all operations of the organization. Therefore, it follows that organizations adopting the MultiCapital Scorecard need to give explicit authority to "every seat in the organization" to contribute to the developmental structure. Sustainable performance demands new rules for new ways of working. The MultiCapital Scorecard process provides the contextual links, but managers within the adopting organizations need to think through the ways in which they can address the transition of thoughts, ideas, and feelings from the inhibiting structure into the developmental structure. They also need to design ways in which it becomes the norm for new ideas to be welcomed, embraced, worked on, and taken seriously.

The developmental structure will become the innovation heart of the self-renewing organization of the future. The MultiCapital Scorecard will be the control system that guides organizations toward sustainable futures for the organizations and their stakeholders in their ever-changing contexts.

When contemplating the challenges ahead for any specific organization, it may help to think through the magnitude of the changes required in the context of the policy model for learning and innovation shown in appendix B (The Sustainability Code). Implementing the eleven "rules" of that code will be a shock to almost every organization in the world. Every organization that wishes to embrace the changes required to move organically from their current unsustainable performance toward a less unsustainable future will need to make it clear to every employee and every contractor that all eleven rules are permitted behavior. That will require the sort of explicit authority to change the present work-flow rules that Hirschhorn sees emerging from the developmental structure.

If management wishes to stimulate the efficiency of that developmental thinking, it will be essential to prevent the hitherto unauthorized ideas from accumulating in the inhibiting structure. To do this, leaders need to articulate in unambiguous terms that every employee is encouraged to adopt all the eleven rules (albeit in constructive dialogue and within the organizational arrangements provided so to do).

More than articulating the authority to do this, management and directors need to show by their own behavior that this is not just a sideshow. This is for real: a new way of working.

APPENDIX D

The Theory and Use of Context-Based Metrics

The Structure and Semantics of Context-Based Metrics

As an extended implementation of Context-Based Sustainability, the MultiCapital Scorecard features the use of context-based metrics. Unlike more conventional relative or absolute metrics, context-based metrics constitute an alternative way of measuring organizational performance. What differentiates them more than anything else from conventional metrics is the manner in which impacts on vital capitals are compared to norms, standards, or thresholds for what such impacts would have to be in order to be sustainable.

For example, most organizations measure and report their impacts on water resources in relative or absolute terms, such as *gallons consumed per unit of production* (relative) or the *gross volume of water consumed in a year* (absolute). A context-based water metric, by contrast, expresses water consumption in comparison to an organization- or facility-specific allocation of available renewable supplies, in which case such consumption either is greater than (unsustainable) or less than or equal to (sustainable) the allocation. In the case of water consumption, allocations constitute not-to-exceed limits.

Context-based metrics are very often science-based as well, in the sense that the norms, standards, or thresholds they contain are determined by reference to scientific evidence. This is typically true in the case of context-based environmental metrics in which ecological thresholds are determined by reference to the physical and biological sciences (for example, what the climate science says about how far greenhouse gas emissions must be reduced in order to reverse climate change).

More broadly construed, science can also be seen as incorporating the social sciences and even management itself, including accounting. What's important here is that the disciplines we use to specify standards of performance be fact-based (reliably descriptive of the way the world really is, was, or possibly can be). Whether the facts be biological, physical, social, psychological, or economic matters less than that the methodologies we use to define sustainability norms and trajectory targets be rational, relevant, systematic, and nonarbitrary.

All context-based metrics are also ethics-based in the sense that the limits and thresholds built into them are normative. This idea is foundational to both Context-Based Sustainability and the MultiCapital Scorecard and also corresponds to systems scientist Sir Geoffrey Vickers's description of how organizations can and do have strategic impacts, a three-step process:[1]

1. **Making reality judgments.** Organizations first determine what is happening on the ground.
2. **Making value judgments.** Next, organizations evaluate the facts in relation to their values and in their own contexts.
3. **Making instrumental judgments.** Last, organizations decide what actions ought to be taken as a consequence of (1) and (2) above, and then act accordingly.

These three steps deliver context-based sustainability norms in the MultiCapital Scorecard. In other words, by combining methodology with the conceptual underpinnings explained throughout the book, we end up with standards of performance that don't just describe possible states of affairs, but which argue instead that such possible states of affairs *ought to be actively embraced* as a regulative ideal for performance—sustainability norms. And those are value claims, not just descriptive ones, as our use of the word *ought* makes clear.

The Normative Basis of Context-Based Metrics

Generally speaking, the approach we take in the MultiCapital Scorecard for specifying sustainability norms and trajectory targets follows the ethical principle known as the categorical imperative put forward by Immanuel Kant in 1785. In Kant's (translated) words, the categorical imperative reads as follows: "There is therefore but one categorical imperative, namely, this: Act only on that maxim whereby thou canst at the same time will that it should become a universal law."[2]

In other words, the correct moral course of action is always one which, if everybody did it, would lead to a fair, just, and equitable world—or to a sustainable world. Others have also relied on the categorical imperative, or at least the same basic idea, as a basis for making their own arguments, including ecological economist Herman Daly, who wrote:

> An overdeveloped country might be defined as one whose level of per capita resource consumption is such that if generalized to all countries [i.e., as a maxim, to use Kant's term] could not be sustained indefinitely; correspondingly an underdeveloped country would be one whose per capita resource consumption is less than what could be sustained indefinitely if all the world consumed at that level [or in other words, if everybody did it].[3]

Calculating one's ecological footprint, too, is predicated on the same *what if everybody did it* ethic to the extent that it measures and reports national impacts on natural capital in terms that are generalized to the world as a way of determining whether or not such impacts are sustainable, and if not, by how much.[4] From this perspective, we can say that sustainability is the subject of a social science that studies, and strives to manage, human impacts on vital capitals relative to norms or standards for what such impacts ought to be in order to ensure human well-being.[5]

In specifying sustainability norms and trajectory targets for an individual organization in the MultiCapital Scorecard, then, it must be the case that if everyone else in the population responsible for maintaining a vital capital were to follow the same rules when specifying their own, the carrying capacity of the vital capital involved would be maintained at a sufficient level. This is the ethical principle we adhere to, the origin of which is grounded in Kantian epistemology.

How to Specify Context-Based Metrics

As discussed above, context-based metrics are measurement models that compare organizations' impacts on vital capitals to standards of performance, or norms, for what such impacts would have to be in order to be sustainable. But this need only be done, of course, for areas of impact that have been determined to be material, as explained in chapter 7. That said, the specification of context-based metrics generally follows a five-step process.

Step one. Sustainability norms must be expressed in terms of what the associated impacts on vital capitals should be. For something like workplace safety, for example, a workplace is obviously a form of constructed capital, the safety of which also requires sustained investments in human and social capitals (for example, to train workers on safety procedures, maintain facilities management teams, and so on). The norms we should be defining for workplace safety, then, are minimum, not-to-fall-below standards, most likely consisting of physical workplace features (for example, clean air, sanitation facilities, fire suppression systems, and so on), training certifications for employees, and plant management standards.

Step two. Next comes the establishment of carrying capacity for these capitals. Sticking with workplace safety as an example, the carrying capacity of interest would be for the constructed, human, and social capitals involved, and in particular for what the levels of such capitals must be in order to ensure employee well-being. *How much of each would be enough to be sustainable?*

Determining the relevant carrying capacities for nonanthropogenic, natural capitals follows a similar line of thought, albeit with one big exception. Rather than setting out to determine how big a stock of capital a given population requires, we set out to determine how big a population a given stock of capital can support. Thus, whereas in the case of constructed, human, social, and economic capitals sustainability boils down to how well we may or may not be producing or maintaining them at sufficient levels, in the case of natural capitals it boils down to how well we may or may not be living within our ecological means.[6]

The carrying capacity of a school system, for example, can be expressed in terms of what the size of a student population is that it can support. Our job as a society is to produce and maintain school systems at levels that are at least sufficient to meet our children's needs. Failing to do so is unsustainable because it puts human well-being at risk. School systems, in turn, are composed of multiple forms of anthropogenic capitals: human, social, constructed, and economic. The same can be said for hospitals, governments, militaries, and other social institutions that are required to meet basic human needs. And all of this can and should be quantified in cases where the capitals involved correspond to an organization's material areas of impact.

Step three. Once the carrying capacities of relevant capitals have been determined for material areas of impact, the next question to consider is who the responsible populations are for maintaining them (either by living within them in the case of natural capitals or continually producing them in the case of the others).

The options here are typically twofold. Either an organization has sole responsibility for maintaining a vital capital (for example, for paying its workers a livable wage or maintaining the safety of a workplace), or else it shares the responsibility with a broader population (for example, the population in a watershed that is co-responsible for maintaining the viability and integrity of water resources therein).

In the case of a capital impact for which an organization is solely responsible, the implication is fairly clear-cut in terms of how that translates into a sustainability norm for a context-based metric. In that case, a threshold for livable wages paid to employees, for example, would figure into a firm's context-based livable wage metric. Let's say the wage is $25. The organization would then determine what the lowest wage *actually* paid to any employee is. As long as the actual lowest wage paid is greater than $25, the organization's performance for the livable wage area of impact would be sustainable.

Impacts on other vital capitals for which the organization shares a responsibility to maintain the capitals involved with others are, of course, more challenging to address, but by no means intractable.

Step four. In cases where the responsible populations for maintaining vital capitals of material relevance to an organization's own performance are extensive (for example, involving surrounding communities or even the global population at large), the critical issue of fair, just, and proportionate allocations must be resolved. For discussion purposes, we and others sometimes refer to this as the *allocation* issue.

Two common examples come rushing to mind here, both of which have been successfully addressed in multiple Context-Based Sustainability and MultiCapital Scorecard projects in the past: (1) impacts on water resources and (2) impacts on the climate system. In both cases, any one organization or facility is having impacts on shared resources, the responsibility for which obviously rests with a broader population: the population in a watershed in the first case and the global population of humans in the second. Fully vetted and robust context-based metrics for each of these two areas of impact now exist and are freely available.

Before explaining allocation further, it is important for us to acknowledge that there are no standards for this. Indeed, the entire corpus of Context-Based Sustainability and the MultiCapital Scorecard is discretionary insofar as whether or not either should be used to measure, manage, and report the performance of organizations except to say that context-based approaches to all of this are explicitly called for by two important international standards: the Global Reporting Initiative and the Global Initiative for Sustainability Ratings (GISR). The International Integrated Reporting Council's Integrated Reporting Framework (<IR> Framework) also calls for such processes to be multiple capital-based, as does the GISR. Still, with the exception of a few countries around the world, all of this is purely voluntary.

None of that, however, is to say that organizations who choose to use the MultiCapital Scorecard cannot independently arrive at sustainability standards of performance, or sustainability norms, that are meaningful, useful, and defensible. Indeed they can, and perhaps even do so in ways that will drive the determination of related standards later on. Here we feel compelled to once again quote the words of Donella Meadows on this subject, who in 1998 wrote:

> It is tempting, given all the caveats and challenges . . . in every report on sustainable development indicators, to be daunted, to postpone the task, to wait for more thinking, more modeling, more agreement—to wait for perfection. While we are waiting for perfection, fisheries are collapsing, greenhouse gases are accumulating, species are disappearing, soils are eroding, forests are overcut, people are suffering. So it is important to get some preliminary indicators out there and into use, the best we can do at the moment. That way, as long as we are willing to evaluate and make corrections, we can start to learn, which is the only way we can ever achieve sustainable development.[7]

In our own use of context-based water and carbon metrics, we have devised two ways of making fair, just, and proportionate allocations of the shared responsibility to maintain the capitals involved (water and the climate system, respectively). One is on a per capita basis, the other is in terms of an organization's proportionate contributions to the economy as represented by gross domestic product (GDP). Both are imperfect and even controversial in some cases, but both also work extremely well and are far better than not making context-based allocations at all. Here we will only describe the two allocation approaches briefly, and would otherwise refer readers to the 2012 book co-authored by one of us, *Corporate Sustainability Management* (McElroy and Van Engelen), in which the mechanics of constructing context-based metrics are described in much greater detail:[8]

Per capita allocations. Once the carrying capacity of a vital capital has been determined (what we sometimes refer to as a *threshold*), fair, just, and proportionate allocations of either the resources involved (natural capitals) or the burden to maintain them (anthropogenic capitals) can be made. The per capita approach to doing so is to determine what the proportionate size of an organization is relative to the overall size of the responsible population.

We can make this calculation by first determining what the overall size of the responsible population is, followed by then determining what the size of the organization is in terms of its workforce size. But since a workforce only inhabits an organization on a part-time basis, we need to convert its part-time presence to what we call a *per capita equivalent* size. To do this, we take total hours worked in a year by a workforce and then divide it by the total number of hours in a year (8,760).

So a workforce, for example, that recorded 500,000 hours on the job in a year would equate to a per capital equivalent of just over 57 people. Note that total headcount in this example might be closer to 250 employees, but once we apply the per capita equivalent conversion, it reduces to 57.

Economic allocations. The other approach we've used to make allocations is by reference to an organization's contributions to GDP. This tends to result in higher entitlements to natural resource use, which in turn some feel is more appropriate given the role companies play in addressing the needs and wants of society. (We nevertheless acknowledge the imperfections of GDP as a universally acceptable or appropriate metric or proxy for making allocations.)

In this case, we start by determining what the overall size of GDP is in the geography or population of interest. In the case of impacts on the climate system, for example, the geography is the world. Or it may be a subset of the world, such as OECD countries, where standards for reducing greenhouse gas emissions may be more stringent in some cases. In either case, we would need source data regarding the size of GDP in the region of interest.

Next we determine what an organization's or facility's contributions to GDP were in the time periods and regions of interest. This typically equates to a company's gross margins or value added (which can be calculated as gross sales minus the cost of goods sold [COGS], where COGS does not include payroll and benefits costs).

Thus, if a company's contribution to GDP in a water basin were 1 percent, it would be entitled to use no more than 1 percent of the available renewable water in a given year.

Once fair, just, and proportionate allocations of either vital capital resources (natural capitals) or the burden to maintain them (anthropogenic capitals) have been made, the results are used to populate norms in their corresponding context-based metrics. Actual measures of impacts on the same capitals can then be taken and compared to the norms.

Once this has been done, variances can be computed and subsequently used to determine the organization's progression performance relative to the sustainability norms and trajectory targets defined for each area of impact. Progression performance scores, in turn, can then be entered into the organization's MultiCapital Scorecard and tallied up therein for the period of interest.

Two Examples of Context-Based Metrics

Two examples involving the construction of context-based metrics for the water and climate impacts cited above will perhaps be useful here.

Water

In all cases where we are assessing the sustainability of water use, there are typically other responsible parties involved, so the allocation issue immediately arises. But before we get to that, it is first important to determine how much renewable water is available in a region of interest. In the case of water, such regions are best expressed in terms of watersheds or basins. We therefore start by determining the physical location of a user or facility and then turn to the geographic or Earth sciences for an understanding of what the contextually relevant watershed is. This data is readily and publicly available for the United States in the form of geographic information systems (GIS) datasets, which is why we always use a GIS system to do context-based water assessments.

Once we've determined what the contextually relevant watershed is, we then expand our use of GIS to determine how much precipitation occurs annually in the watershed of interest. Here again, this data tends to be readily available, also in a GIS format.

Next comes an effort to determine what the size of the population is in the same watershed of interest. Again, this data, too, tends to be readily available in GIS form. And if the allocation method we ultimately intend to use is the economic one, we also need to determine what the size of GDP is in the same area; that, too, tends to be available in GIS form.

Turning next to the meteorological and climate sciences, we then take total annual precipitation and subtract at least half of it because of evapotranspiration. We then allocate half of the remainder (a quarter of the starting amount) to ecological functions. The remaining half (or quarter of we started with) is then allocated to households and domestic use in the watershed using accepted standards for that. And then finally we allocate the remaining renewable supplies to organizations according to their proportionate contributions to GDP.[9]

Note that at no time under this approach do we treat surface or groundwater supplies or quantities as being available in our allocations. Instead, all of our allocations are confined to renewable flows only, which flow through watersheds by way of precipitation, evapotranspiration, consumption, and discharge. Ours is a very conservative approach indeed.

The Climate System

Here again we rely very heavily on science, which in the case of impacts on the climate system obviously involves climate science. Of particular interest to us here are climate change mitigation scenarios developed by climate scientists that specify levels of reduction in anthropogenic greenhouse gas emissions that must be achieved in order for climate change to be reversed.[10]

Unlike water use, which we tend to look at on a year-by-year basis, our assessments of organizational performance relative to impacts on the climate system are both annual and cumulative over multiyear periods of time. This is because of the way the climate science calls for reductions—progressively over time as opposed to all at once.

In general, what we do, then, is apply a pattern of science-based greenhouse gas reductions to an organization's own emissions, as if the organization were the only emitter of greenhouse gases on Earth. If all organizations and emitters did this, the science-based mitigation scenario at the global level would theoretically be achieved. In any case, an organization can only be held responsible for its own emissions, and it seems appropriate to set targets for reducing its emissions, therefore, in accordance with what the climate science is calling for.

Since the context-based carbon metrics we use to do all of this are applied on a multiyear basis, they must also take into account that both organizations and the economies in which they operate are constantly changing in size. Our metric accounts for this on the fly, such that allocations of entitlements to emit according to a firm's contributions to GDP are accurately calculated each year, but always in a way that allowable emissions in the aggregate never add up to more than what the science-based scenario we're using permits.

A Final Note on Individual vs. Collective Accountability

Observers of Context-Based Sustainability and its use of context-based metrics sometimes make the mistake of confusing its focus on individual accountability with collective accountability. When we say, for example, that an organization's fair, just, and proportionate share of available renewable water is X, such an allocation has nothing to do with whether or not everyone else in the same watershed is abiding by their own allocations. Rather, the allocations we defined are intended to indicate what an organization's own specific duty is to operate in a sustainable way.

Thus, an organization's fair, just, and proportionate share of water resources is not at all influenced by whether others are abiding by theirs. Rather, what Context-Based Sustainability sets out to do is specify an organization's own individual accountability and then measure performance against it, regardless of whether others in the same contextually relevant arena are adhering to theirs.

APPENDIX E

Accounting Adjustments Recommended for the MultiCapital Scorecard

B ased on financial reporting standards commonly applied to commercial enterprises, the following adjustments are recommended to adjust the income statement (P&L) and balance sheet to reflect their real terms residual income. They are not mandatory, but they offer the reporting entity a toolkit of techniques that may be appropriate to their circumstances to bring reported financials closer to the underlying reality within their own context.

One principle of sustainability must be that the resources used in the reporting process should be commensurate to the size, scale, complexity, and viability of the organization. In the early 2010s it is safe to say that few if any organizations are operating in a truly sustainable way on all capitals. It is not the intention of the multicapitals approach to put them out of business, but instead the multicapitals approach attempts to highlight ways in which they can reduce their degree of unsustainability and move toward true sustainability in the most effective and efficient way. Consequently, the learning process may only have the resources to start on a relatively small scale. Resources are part of the contextual conditions that leaders must contemplate in establishing the scope of their sustainability ambition.

The following recommended adjustments are written as if the choice has been made to adopt them and the resources to do so properly are available.

Adjust Historic Costs to Real Terms

Historic cost accounting conventions have operated for more than five centuries as the normal basis of stewardship accounting. These are the transactional costs: the money spent in buying the asset. They remain in use today; indeed, lay people often think of them as "actual costs." However, they fail to maintain monetary capital intact in times of rising prices and devaluing currencies. Since the principles of the MultiCapital Scorecard are based on maintaining the carrying capacity of vital capitals, it is consistent to apply the same principles to the maintenance of economic capitals for multicapitalism.

There are several ways to adjust historic costs to maintain economic capital in times of inflation and devaluation, mostly depending on which concept of *capital* is to be maintained:

- One capital concept is preserving the spending power of the monetary value of the originally invested funds subscribed by investing stakeholders (or the price at which investors bought their shares).
- Another requires preserving the operating capacity of the land, plant, and equipment purchased with those funds over the years.
- Yet another concept demands maintaining the capacity of the whole organization to earn the stream of income that those first two capital concepts have generated in practice in recent years.
- A fourth capital concept argues that the only asset value that is meaningful once the organization has been set up is its realizable value if it were to be sold as a whole or in pieces.

Of these four concepts of economic capital maintenance, it would seem that the concept most consistent with the principles of carrying capacity maintenance (which lies at the heart of the MultiCapital Scorecard) is preserving the operating capacity of the organization. This is termed *current replacement cost*. It requires three basic adjustments:

- Adjust asset and liability values to current replacement costs
- Adjust depreciation, amortization, and other material costs to replacement cost
- Correct prior year comparatives to reflect the elasticity of the measuring stick (currency value)

There is rich literature and deep experience of inflation accounting to support the necessary adjustments. There is also a wide range of opinions about the validity of each and the most appropriate means of calculating them. It is not the purpose of this book either to enter into the detail or to mediate between opposing views on the subject of accounting for inflation impacts on financial capital. Suffice it to say that the more that sustainability thinking contemplates longer time horizons (than conventional performance reporting), the more it needs to avoid the distortions that result from ignoring the impact of inflation on economic performance measurement.

We believe that for the purposes of implementing a multicapitals approach to income determination, an organization should select the most appropriate capital and income determination principles for its circumstances and apply them consistently over a number of years. The review processes built into the MultiCapital Scorecard approach should extend to reviewing the continuing suitability of the accounting principles being used. Such is the nature of continuous improvement in a learning organization.

Reflect Real but Unrealized Capital Holding Gains in P&L and Balance Sheet

The economic return from many operations arises not only from the income stream it creates, but also (sometimes mainly) from the real terms increase in the value of the assets it holds. One typical example is in farming communities where operations may continue to make losses year after year, but where the land increases steadily in value.

Whereas traditional accounting concepts have developed "cautionary principles" to asset valuations that provide for reductions in their value in cases where market values reduce, there is no corresponding obligation to recognize increased capital valuation when values increase above their real terms book values.

Thus losses on assets held may be written off and reduce the reported income, whereas real terms value increases escape notice. The result of this skewed valuation principle is that gains from holding assets are only taken into the accounts when such assets are sold and the income from the sale is realized.

There are strong arguments for making this principle even-handed in management accounts by taking account of the real terms material increase or decrease in capital values whether or not they are realized.

Incorporate the Valuation of Intangible Assets in P&L and Balance Sheet

There are currently obligations placed on organizations that have acquired businesses to reflect the intangible asset values (such as brand values) on their balance sheets. Consequently, their income statements are reduced by the depreciation of such asset values or by any impairment the asset values may suffer.

No such obligations are placed on the intangible assets created by organizations internally. Whereas the mere valuation and accounting treatment for intangible assets does not on its own ensure that their values are indeed maintained, the unbalanced accounting treatment needs to be corrected if comparable MultiCapital Scorecard statements of economic value creation are to be prepared within divisions of a single reporting unit. (See the section on global brand values in chapter 8 for a fuller discussion of brand value creation and its accounting consequences.)

We argue in favor of recognizing all tangible and intangible capital assets and reflecting in the financial performance all increases or decreases to them. This does not detract from the duty of organizations to attend to the requirements to manage the factors that drive those values up or down. Indeed, the essence of the multicapitals approach is to attend to such capitals.

This raises the issue of whether it is double counting to recognize a social asset in the social bottom line and also to do so in the economic capital bottom line. We believe that such double counting should be eliminated as far as is possible.

Whether the capital value creation (or destruction) should be classified as social, environmental, or economic calls for judgment by management. We consider this classification issue to be of lesser importance than capturing all value creation (or destruction) wherever it may arise.

As accounting techniques develop and data sources to support the valuation of intangibles improve, it may be expected that the incorporation of intangible capital values into the financial performance of organizations of all sorts will increase. It would be a natural progression resulting from their widening recognition and should therefore be welcomed.

Incorporate the Financial Impacts of Social and Environmental Externalities

The environmental profit and loss accounts (E P&L) produced by PUMA in 2011 made a serious effort to capture and evaluate the social and environmental external costs caused by PUMA and its suppliers.[1] These costs fell outside the boundaries that are considered by traditional financial accounting techniques. PUMA estimated the total of such unaccounted costs to amount to approximately the same quantum as the net income it reported in the year in question. However, only about 10 percent of the total cost would have been attributable to PUMA itself within its own reporting boundaries. The rest would have fallen to the suppliers' activities and therefore to their accounts (taking the very short term and narrow view of where they would have fallen).

Nevertheless, consumers of PUMA's products for that year paid some €140 million less than the full environmentally and socially complete costs incurred in making those products. This also means that environmental and social capitals in PUMA and its supply chain were probably depleted by a similar amount. This was a pilot project and made no pretense to be beyond contest.

We encourage organizations to calculate and account for the full environmental and social costs they or others incur in their annual running costs. Even when this is done, however, it remains a job half done (at best). The other half of the job is to attend to what is needed in the real world (as opposed to the financial world) to maintain and preserve the vital capitals. That is exactly what the MultiCapital Scorecard requires. That requirement is no greater nor lesser as a result of incorporating financial estimates of the values of services and capitals provided in the economic analysis of performance.

Of course, to those stakeholders whose concerns are purely financial, E P&L sounds a loud warning bell. But the warning bell should not be confused with the action of putting out the fires. The MultiCapital Scorecard indicates exactly where the fire is burning the world's existing capitals (often unnoticed).

NOTES

Introduction

1. The *triple bottom line* is a term coined by John Elkington (1997), by which he meant to refer to three dimensions of organizational performance: financial, social, and environmental. The idea behind it, however, can be traced as far back as 1713, in what was perhaps the first book ever written on sustainability management and accounting: Hans Carl von Carlowitz, *Sylvicultura Oeconomica* (Leipzig: Johann Friedrich Brauns, 1713).

2. Mark W. McElroy and Jo M. L. van Engelen, *Corporate Sustainability Management: The Art and Science of Managing Non-Financial Performance* (London: Routledge, 2012).

3. In her seminal monograph, *Indicators and Information Systems for Sustainable Development*, Donella H. Meadows wrote: "It is tempting, given all the caveats and challenges . . . in every report on sustainable development indicators, to be daunted, to postpone the task, to wait for more thinking, more modeling, more agreement—to wait for perfection. While we are waiting for perfection, fisheries are collapsing, greenhouse gases are accumulating, species are disappearing, soils are eroding, forests are overcut, people are suffering. So it is important to get some preliminary indicators out there and into use, the best we can do at the moment. That way, as long as we are willing to evaluate and make corrections, we can start to learn, which is the only way we can ever achieve sustainable development." Donella H. Meadows, *Indicators and Information Systems for Sustainable Development* (Hartland, VT: The Sustainability Institute, 1998), accessed March 25, 2016, http://donellameadows.org/wp-content/userfiles/IndicatorsInformation.pdf.

Chapter One:
An Overview of the MultiCapital Scorecard

1. Readers interested in obtaining an extensive bibliography of significant works on the capital theory basis of sustainability will find one here: http://www.sustainable organizations.org/Capital-Theory-References.pdf.

Notes

2. For more information about the Panama Papers leaked in April 2016, see: *Wikipedia*, "Panama Papars," last modified June 14, 2016, https://en.wikipedia.org/wiki/Panama _Papers.

3. Martin P. Thomas, "Scenarios towards Social Dialogue," in *Business Planning for Turbulent Times*, eds. Rafael Ramirez, John W. Selsky, and Kees van der Heijden (London: Earthscan, 2008), chap. 9.

4. This quote is from a speech given by Professor Leon G. Megginson of Louisiana State University at the convention of the Southwestern Social Science Association in 1963. The text of his address was published in the quarterly journal of the association. The quote we have used is sometimes incorrectly misattributed, in whole or in part, to Charles Darwin himself.

5. For a good discussion on the important distinction between duties and obligations, see John Rawls, *A Theory of Justice* (Cambridge, MA: Harvard University Press, 1971), chap. 6.

6. "Barclays Boss Admits It Could Take 10 Years to Rebuild Public Trust," *The Guardian*, accessed April 3, 2016, http://www.theguardian.com/business/2013/dec/31/barclays -antony-jenkins-trust-ppi-libor.

7. "Enabling Business Decisions That Integrate Natural Capital: Learning from a Complex Systems Perspective," The Natural Capital Coalition, accessed March 29, 2016, http:// www.naturalcapitalcoalition.org/js/plugins/filemanager/files/019750_NCC_White _Paper_Draft29.pdf.

8. Gill G. Ringland, Oliver Sparrow, and Patricia Lustig, *Beyond Crisis: Achieving Renewal in a Turbulent World* (Chichester West Sussex: John Wiley and Sons, 2010), 101.

9. "The 2016 Sustainability Leaders," GlobeScan and SustainAbility, accessed June 24, 2016, http://www.globescan.com/component/edocman/?view=document &id=250&Itemid=591

10. "Try Reality," Robert Wood Johnson, Johnson & Johnson Services, accessed March 28, 2016, http://www.kilmerhouse.com/2013/12/the-writing-of-our-credo.

11. Ronald Inglehart and Christian Welzel, *Modernization, Cultural Change, and Democracy: The Human Development Sequence* (Cambridge, UK: Cambridge University Press, 2005), 99.

12. "Code of Conduct," The Volkswagen Group, accessed March 28, 2016, http://en .volkswagen.com/content/medialib/vwd4/de/Volkswagen/Nachhaltigkeit/service /download/corporate_governance/Code_of_Conduct/_jcr_content/renditions /rendition.file/the-volkswagen-group-code-of-conduct.pdf.

13. Reputation Dividend's website and publications can be found at http://www.reputation dividend.com.

14. Apple's 2014 CSR reputation contribution was reported privately to the authors on the basis of data otherwise reported in Reputation Dividend's report: "The 2015 U.S. Reputation Dividend Report," Reputation Dividend, accessed March 28, 2016, http:// www.reputationdividend.com/files/1514/3515/4447/US_2015_Reputation_Dividend _Report_-_Final.pdf.

15. "Environmental Responsibility Report: 2014 Progress Report, Covering FY2013," Apple Computer, accessed March 28, 2016, https://www.apple.com/environment/pdf /Apple_Environmental_Responsibility_Report_2014.pdf.

16. These companies' CSR reputation contributions were reported privately to the authors on the basis of data otherwise reported in Reputation Dividend's report: "The 2015 U.S. Reputation Dividend Report," Reputation Dividend, accessed March 28, 2016, http:// www.reputationdividend.com/files/1514/3515/4447/US_2015_Reputation _Dividend_Report_-_Final.pdf.

17. "The International <IR> Framework," International Integrated Reporting Council, December 2013, accessed March 28, 2016, http://integratedreporting.org/wp-content/uploads/2015/03/13-12-08-THE-INTERNATIONAL-IR-FRAMEWORK-2-1.pdf.

18. "King Code of Governance Principles for South Africa 2009," Institute of Directors Southern Africa, 2009, accessed March 28, 2016, http://c.ymcdn.com/sites/www.iodsa.co.za/resource/collection/94445006-4F18-4335-B7FB-7F5A8B23FB3F/King_III_Code_for_Governance_Principles_.pdf.

Chapter Two:
Vital Capitals and the MultiCapital Scorecard

1. For several examples of this particular interpretation of capital, see Irving Fisher, *The Nature of Capital and Income* (San Diego: Simon Publications,1906); Kenneth E. Boulding, "Income or Welfare," *The Review of Economic Studies* 17, no. 2 (1949): 77–86; Robert Costanza and Herman Daly, "Natural Capital and Sustainable Development," *Conservation Biology* 6, no. 1 (1992): 37–46; Paul Ekins, "A Four-Capital Model of Wealth Creation," in *Real-Life Economics: Understanding Wealth Creation*, eds. Paul Ekins and Manfred Max-Neef (London: Routledge, 1992), 147–155; Mathis Wackernagel and William Rees, *Our Ecological Footprint: Reducing Human Impact on the Earth* (Gabriola Island, BC, Canada: New Society Publishers, 1996); Robert Costanza et al., *An Introduction to Ecological Economics* (Boca Raton, FL: CRC Press LLC, 1997); Jonathan Porritt, *Capitalism as if the World Matters* (London: Earthscan, 2005); Mark W. McElroy, *Social Footprints: Measuring the Social Sustainability Performance of Organizations*, PhD diss. (Groningen, The Netherlands: University of Groningen, 2008); Joseph Stiglitz, Amartya Sen, and Jean-Paul Fitoussi, *Mis-Measuring Our Lives: Why GDP Doesn't Add Up* (New York: The New Press, 2010); and Mark W. McElroy and Jo M. L. van Engelen, *Corporate Sustainability Management: The Art and Science of Managing Non-Financial Performance* (London: Routledge, 2012).

2. Costanza and Daly, "Natural Capital and Sustainable Development," p. 38.

3. Various multiple capital models have been put forward over the years, including Ekins's four-capital model (Ekins, "A Four-Capital Model of Wealth Creation"), Jonathon Porritt's five capitals framework (Porritt, *Capitalism as if the World Matters*), the IIRC's six capitals (Martin P. Thomas, "Performance That Lasts: How Leading Organisations Measure Performance in 2050," in *New Eyes: The Human Side of Leadership*, eds. Joanne Flinn, Roberto Saco, Mike Staresinic, and Dan Ballbach [London: The Change Leaders, 2013], 39–58), and our own five-capitals model in which intellectual capital is not explicitly listed and instead is considered to be embedded in most of the other five (see figure 2.1). For an excellent account of the growing importance of multiple capital frameworks to performance measurement and reporting, see Jane Gleeson-White, *Six Capitals, or Can Accountants Save the Planet?* (New York: W. W. Norton & Company, 2015).

4. The Center for Sustainable Organizations's context-based carbon metric is freely downloadable at http://www.sustainableorganizations.org/context-based-metrics-in-public-domain.html.

Chapter Three:
Putting the MultiCapital Scorecard into Practice

1. John Rawls, *A Theory of Justice* (Cambridge, MA: Harvard University Press, 1971), 98.

2. For examples of previously developed context-based metrics, see McElroy, *Social Footprints*; McElroy and Van Engelen, *Corporate Sustainability Management*; and the Center for Sustainable Organizations at http://www.sustainableorganizations.org /context-based-metrics-in-public-domain.html.

3. Meadows, *Indicators and Information Systems*.

4. For more information on the concept of duties and obligations, see Rawls, *A Theory of Justice*, 293–343; McElroy, *Social Footprints*, 220; and McElroy and Van Engelen, *Corporate Sustainability Management*, 110–114.

5. For more on how materiality is handled in the MultiCapital Scorecard, see Thomas & McElroy, LLC, "MultiCapital Scorecard: Rethinking Organizational Performance," 2015, accessed June 14, 2016, http://www.multicapitalscorecard.com/wp-content /uploads/2015/01/Materiality_in_MCS.pdf.

6. This perspective on self-determined materiality has been separately argued by McElroy and Van Engelen, *Corporate Sustainability Management*; Robert G. Eccles, Michael P. Krzus, and Sydney Ribot, *The Integrated Reporting Movement: Meaning, Momentum, Motives, and Materiality* (Hoboken, NJ: John Wiley and Sons, 2015); and Mark W. McElroy and Martin P. Thomas, "The MultiCapital Scorecard," *Sustainability Accounting Management and Policy Journal* 6, no. 3 (2015): 425–438.

7. This conception of correlating impacts on specific capitals with the "bottom lines" they correspond to was arguably first put forward by John Elkington, *Cannibals with Forks: The Triple Bottom Line of 21st Century Business* (Oxford, UK: Capstone Publishing Limited, 1997), and then later taken up and operationalized by McElroy and Van Engelen, *Corporate Sustainability Management*, and McElroy and Thomas, "The MultiCapital Scorecard."

Chapter Four:
Financial Capitals in the MultiCapital Scorecard

1. Franco Modigliani and Merton H. Miller, "The Cost of Capital, Corporation Finance and the Theory of Investment," *The American Economic Review* 48, no. 3 (1958): 261–297.

2. Alfred Marshall, *Principles of Economics* (London: Macmillan and Co., 1890).

3. Edgar O. Edwards and Philip W. Bell, *The Theory and Measurement of Business Income* (Berkeley, CA: University of California Press, 1961); and David Solomons, *Divisional Performance Measurement and Control* (New York: Financial Executives Research Foundation, 1965).

4. Clive R. Emmanuel and David T. Otley, "The Usefulness of Residual Income," *Journal of Business Finance & Accounting* 3, no. 4 (1976): 43–51.

5. Peter F. Drucker, "The Information Executives Truly Need," *Harvard Business Review*, January–February 1995, accessed April 3, 2016, https://hbr.org/1995/01/the -information-executives-truly-need.

6. More about economic value added can be found at Ben McClure, "All About EVA," Investopedia, http://www.investopedia.com/articles/fundamental/03/031203.asp; more about Stern Stewart & Co. can be found at http://www.sternstewart.com.

Chapter Seven: Materiality

1. More about SustainAbility's conception of *one materiality* can be found in a report of theirs issued in December of 2014 entitled, "See Change: How Transparency Drives

Performance," a copy of which can be downloaded from http://www.sustainability
.com/library/see-change#.VvreEzYhxGM (accessed June 14, 2016).

Chapter Eight: Intangibles

1. Charles Tilley, "CIMA CEO Column," *Financial Management*, June 2015, 40, accessed June 29, 2016, http://fmapp.cimaglobal.com/seven/financialprototype/index.html #issue/june2015/portrait/40.
2. PwC, "Technological Breakthroughs," accessed June 14, 2016, http://www.pwc.co.uk /issues/megatrends/technological-breakthroughs.html.
3. Attributed to Mr. Allen by Charles Tilley, CEO of CIMA, in a presentation he gave at the CIMA regional meeting at the Hilton Cobham on November 25, 2015, titled "Integrated Reporting: Better Business, Better Society."
4. Simon Cole is a co-founding partner at the UK consultancy Reputation Dividend, whose pioneering work in the area of attributing the contributions of corporate reputations to their market value is highly relevant to the MultiCapital Scorecard.
5. Simon Cole, "The Impact of Reputation on Market Value," *World Economics* 13, no. 3 (2012): 47–68, accessed March 29, 2016, http://www.reputationdividend.com/files /4713/4822/1479/Reputation_Dividend_WEC_133_Cole.pdf.

Chapter Nine: Other Key Issues

1. Hans Carl von Carlowitz, *Sylvicultura Oeconomica* (Leipzig: Johann Friedrich Brauns, 1713).
2. Martin P. Thomas, "Performance That Lasts: How Leading Organisations Measure Performance in 2050," in *New Eyes: The Human Side of Leadership*, eds. Joanne Flinn, Roberto Saco, Mike Staresinic, and Dan Ballbach (London: The Change Leaders, 2013), 39–58.
3. United Nations Environment Programme, *Raising the Bar—Advancing Environmental Disclosure in Sustainability Reporting* (Paris: UNEP, 2015); also available for download at http://www.unep.org/NewsCentre/default.aspx?DocumentID=26854&ArticleID =35553.
4. GRI: https://www.globalreporting.org/Pages/default.aspx; IIRC: http://integrated reporting.org; Robert G. Eccles and Michael P. Krzus, *One Report: Integrated Reporting for a Sustainable Strategy* (Hoboken, NJ: John Wiley and Sons, 2010); UNEP: http://www .unep.org/NewsCentre/default.aspx?DocumentID=26854&ArticleID=35553.
5. More information about the G4 reporting standard can be found on the GRI website: https://www.globalreporting.org/standards/Pages/default.aspx.
6. More information about the Sustainability Context Group can be found on their website at http://www.sustycontext.org; in addition, the text of comments submitted by the Sustainability Context Group to the Global Reporting Initiative during the public comment period as G4 was being developed (September 24, 2012) can be found here: http://www.sustainableorganizations.org/SCG-GRI-G4-Comment-Submitted-9-24 -12.pdf.
7. Excerpted from the GRI website under a subheading that reads "GRI and IIRC" here: https://www.globalreporting.org/information/current-priorities/integrated-reporting /Pages/default.aspx.

Notes

8. "G4 Sustainability Reporting Guidelines," Global Reporting Initiative, accessed August 25, 2016, https://www.globalreporting.org/resourcelibrary/GRIG4-Part1-Reporting -Principles-and-Standard-Disclosures.pdf.

9. GRI's G4 sustainability reporting guidelines are freely downloadable from GRI's website at https://www.globalreporting.org/standards/g4/Pages/default.aspx.

10. Eccles and Krzus, *One Report*, 109.

11. Ibid.,148–156.

12. Ibid., 170–176.

13. UNEP, *Raising the Bar*, 52.

14. Ibid.

15. Eccles, Krzus, and Ribot, *The Integrated Reporting Movement*, 109.

16. For more information about the meaning of "integrated thinking," see http://www .integratedreportingsa.org/IntegratedThinking.aspx; http://www.accountingfor sustainability.org/integrated-thinking/10-main-elements-to-embed-sustainability; and https://www.ifac.org/publications-resources/creating-value-integrated-thinking; and also Eccles, Krzus, and Ribot, *The Integrated Reporting Movement*, 8.

17. Eccles, Krzus, and Ribot, *The Integrated Reporting Movement*, 47; and "Framework for Integrated Reporting and the Integrated Report," Integrated Reporting Committee (IRC) of South Africa, accessed March 30, 2016, http://www.sustainabilitysa.org /Portals/0/IRC%20of%20SA%20Integrated%20Reporting%20Guide%20Jan%2011.pdf.

18. Eccles, Krzus, and Ribot, *The Integrated Reporting Movement*, 47.

19. Ibid., 49.

20. Ibid., 125.

21. Ibid., 151.

22. Gleeson-White, *Six Capitals*, 6–7.

23. Luca Pacioli, *Summa de Arithmetica, Geometria, Proportione, et Proportionalità* (Venice: Paganino de Paganini, 1494).

24. Gleeson-White, *Double Entry*.

25. Gleeson-White, *Six Capitals*, 183.

26. Ibid., 187.

27. Ibid., 216–217.

28. Ibid., 136–137; and Donella H. Meadows, "Leverage Points: Places to Intervene in a System," accessed March 30, 2016, http://donellameadows.org/archives/leverage -points-places-to-intervene-in-a-system/.

29. Fred E. Emery and Eric L. Trist, "The Causal Texture of Organizational Environ- ments," *Human Relations* 18, no. 1 (1965): 21–32.

30. Gleeson-White, *Six Capitals*, 287; and Christopher D. Stone, "Should Trees Have Standing— Toward Legal Rights for Natural Objects," *Southern California Law Review* 45 (1972): 450–487.

31. For more information about the "Valuing Your Talent" initiative in the United Kingdom, see http://www.valuingyourtalent.com/index.

32. Chris Argyris, *Flawed Advice and the Management Trap* (Oxford: Oxford University Press, 2000), 72.

33. Ibid., 157.

34. More information about IRAS can be found on their website at http://www.iras.co.za.

35. World Business Council for Sustainable Development (WBCSD), "Reporting Matters: Redefining Performance and Disclosure, WBCSD 2015 Report," accessed April 1, 2016, http://wbcsdpublications.org/project/reporting-matters-2015.

36. Ibid.

Chapter Ten: Conclusions: Mind the Gaps

1. This chapter was based on a paper written by the authors and presented by Martin P. Thomas at the first WBCSD Environmental and Sustainability Management Accounting Network (EMAN) conference held in October 2015 in Geneva, the proceedings of which can be downloaded at http://eman-eu.org/wp-content/uploads/2016/04/Proceedings_EMAN_2015_Bridging-Corporate-and-Academic-Contributions.pdf.
2. McElroy, *Social Footprints*; McElroy and Van Engelen, *Corporate Sustainability Management*.
3. In addition to Karl R. Popper, *Logic of Scientific Discovery* (New York: Basic Books, 1959); Karl R. Popper, *Conjectures and Refutations* (New York: Basic Books, 1962); Karl R. Popper, *Objective Knowledge—An Evolutionary Approach* (Oxford: Oxford University Press, 1972); and Rawls, *A Theory of Justice*, Context-Based Sustainability and the MultiCapital Scorecard itself are deeply grounded in the capital theory basis of sustainability put forward by the likes of Kenneth E. Boulding, "The Economics of the Coming Spaceship Earth," in *Environmental Quality in a Growing Economy*, ed. Henry Jarrett (Baltimore, MD: The Johns Hopkins Press, 1966); Boulding, "Income or Welfare"; Fisher, *Nature of Capital and Income*; Herman E. Daly, *Beyond Growth: The Economics of Sustainable Development* (Boston, MA: Beacon Press, 1996); Herman E. Daly, *Steady State Economics* (San Francisco, CA: W. H. Freeman and Company, 1977); Costanza et al., *An Introduction to Ecological Economics*; Costanza and Daly, "Natural Capital and Sustainable Development"; Meadows, *Indicators and Information Systems*; Meadows et al., *The Limits to Growth* (New York: New American Library, 1972); Wackernagel and Rees, *Our Ecological Footprint*; and many others. Once again, readers interested in seeing an extensive bibliography of important works on the capital theory basis of sustainability will find one at http://www.sustainableorganizations.org/Capital-Theory-References.pdf.
4. Immanuel Kant, *Groundwork of the Metaphysic of Morals*, trans. T. K. Abbott (Lexington, KY: BN Publishing, 2010).
5. Ringland, Sparrow, and Lustig, *Beyond Crisis*.
6. Ronald Inglehart and Christian Welzel, *Modernization, Cultural Change, and Democracy: The Human Development Sequence* (Cambridge, UK: Cambridge University Press, 2005).
7. From a written endorsement of the MultiCapital Scorecard supplied by Rob Michalak, Global Director of Social Mission, Ben & Jerry's Homemade, Inc. (Unilever).
8. "King Code of Governance Principles for South Africa 2009," Institute of Directors Southern Africa, accessed March 28, 2016, http://c.ymcdn.com/sites/www.iodsa.co.za/resource/collection/94445006-4F18-4335-B7FB-7F5A8B23FB3F/King_III_Code_for_Governance_Principles_.pdf.

Appendix B: The Sustainability Code

1. This paper was the basis of a presentation given by Mark W. McElroy at the 4th ISSS "Innovative Nation: Theory and Practice" conference in Beijing, China, in November 2006.
2. Isaac Asimov, "Runaround," *Astounding Science Fiction*, March 1942, 100.
3. Robert Audi, *Epistemology—A Contemporary Introduction to the Theory of Knowledge* (London: Routledge, 1998).
4. Mark W. McElroy, *The New Knowledge Management: Complexity, Learning, and Sustainable Innovation* (Burlington, MA: Butterworth-Heinemann, 2003).

Notes

5. Popper, *Objective Knowledge*.
6. Joseph M. Firestone, *The Adaptive Crisis and the Foundations of Social Science: A Critique of Empirical Social Science and Some Suggestions for Its Reconstruction* (unpublished manuscript) (Binghamton, NY: State University of New York at Binghamton, 1974).
7. McElroy, *The New Knowledge Management*.
8. Joseph M. Firestone and Mark W. McElroy, *Key Issues in the New Knowledge Management* (Burlington, MA: Butterworth-Heinemann, 2003).
9. John H. Holland, *Hidden Order: How Adaptation Builds Complexity* (Reading, MA: Perseus Books, 1995).
10. Daly, *Beyond Growth*.
11. Holland, *Hidden Order*.
12. Everett W. Hall, *Our Knowledge of Fact and Value* (Chapel Hill: University of North Carolina Press, 1961).

Appendix C:
Larry Hirschhorn's Psychodynamic Framework

1. Ringland, Sparrow, and Lustig, *Beyond Crisis*.
2. Frederick W. Taylor was a late-nineteenth/early-twentieth-century management theoretician best known for his reductionist approach to shop management, which he called "scientific management."

Appendix D:
The Theory and Use of Context-Based Metrics

1. Geoffrey Vickers, *The Art of Judgment: A Study of Policy Making* (London: Chapman & Hall, 1965), chap. 4.
2. Kant, *Groundwork of the Metaphysic of Morals*.
3. Daly, *Beyond Growth*, 106.
4. See Wackernagel and Rees, *Our Ecological Footprint*.
5. McElroy and Van Engelen, *Corporate Sustainability Management*, 37.
6. This line of thought was developed and more fully articulated by Mark McElroy in his PhD dissertation in 2008, in which Context-Based Sustainability was also more broadly defined: McElroy, *Social Footprints*.
7. Meadows, "Indicators and Information Systems."
8. McElroy and Van Engelen, *Corporate Sustainability Management*, chap. 3.
9. This particular approach for making fair, just, and proportionate allocations of renewable water resources to individual organizations was first put forward in 2011, by Dr. Richard W. Stammer, CEO of Agri-Mark, Inc. (doing business as Cabot Creamery Cooperative) as a means of determining the sustainability of water use at his company's manufacturing facilities. More about that case can be found in an article here: http://www.sustainablebrands.com/news_and_views/jan2012/how-leadership-cabot-creamery-makes-all-difference-0.
10. See, for example, the representative concentration pathways (RPCs) at the RCP Database (version 2.100), accessed June 14, 2016, http://tntcat.iiasa.ac.at:8787/RcpDb/dsd?Action=htmlpage&page=welcome.

223

Appendix E: Accounting Adjustments Recommended for the MultiCapital Scorecard

1. More information about environmental profit and loss (E P&L) accounts can be found at *Wikipedia*, "Environmental Profit and Loss Account," last modified September 10, 2015, https://en.wikipedia.org/wiki/Environmental_profit_and_loss_account.

BIBLIOGRAPHY

Argyris, Chris. *Flawed Advice and the Management Trap*. Oxford: Oxford University Press, 2000.

Argyris, Chris. *Overcoming Organizational Defenses*. Upper Saddle River, NJ: Prentice Hall, 1990.

Boulding, Kenneth E. "The Economics of the Coming Spaceship Earth." In *Environmental Quality in a Growing Economy*, ed. Henry Jarrett (Baltimore, MD: The Johns Hopkins Press, 1966).

Boulding, Kenneth E. "Income or Welfare." *The Review of Economic Studies* 17, no. 2 (1949): 77–86.

Cole, Simon. "The Impact of Reputation on Market Value." *World Economics* 13, no. 3 (2012): 47–68, accessed March 29, 2016, http://www.reputationdividend.com/files/4713/4822/1479/Reputation_Dividend_WEC_133_Cole.pdf.

Costanza, Robert, John H. Cumberland, Herman Daly, Richard Goodland, and Richard B. Norgaard. *An Introduction to Ecological Economics*. Boca Raton, FL: CRC Press LLC, 1997.

Costanza, Robert, and Herman Daly. "Natural Capital and Sustainable Development." *Conservation Biology* 6, no. 1 (1992): 37–46.

Daly, Herman E. *Beyond Growth: The Economics of Sustainable Development*. Boston, MA: Beacon Press, 1996.

Daly, Herman E. *Steady State Economics*. San Francisco, CA: W. H. Freeman and Company, 1977.

Eccles, Robert G., and Michael P. Krzus. *One Report: Integrated Reporting for a Sustainable Strategy*. Hoboken, NJ: John Wiley and Sons, 2010.

Eccles, Robert G., Michael P. Krzus, and Sydney Ribot. *The Integrated Reporting Movement: Meaning, Momentum, Motives, and Materiality*. Hoboken, NJ: John Wiley and Sons, 2015.

Edwards, Edgar O., and Philip W. Bell. *The Theory and Measurement of Business Income*. Berkeley: University of California Press, 1961.

Elkington, John. *Cannibals with Forks: The Triple Bottom Line of 21st Century Business*. Oxford, UK: Capstone Publishing Limited, 1997.

Ekins, Paul. "A Four-Capital Model of Wealth Creation." In *Real-Life Economics: Understanding Wealth Creation*, eds. Paul Ekins and Manfred Max-Neef (London: Routledge, 1992).

Emery, Fred E., and Eric L. Trist. "The Causal Texture of Organizational Environments." *Human Relations* 18, no. 1 (1965): 21–32.

Emmanuel, Clive R., and David T. Otley. "The Usefulness of Residual Income." *Journal of Business Finance & Accounting* 3, no. 4 (1976): 43–51.

225

Firestone, Joseph M., and Mark W. McElroy. *Key Issues in the New Knowledge Management*. Burlington, MA: Butterworth-Heinemann, 2003.

Fisher, Irving. *The Nature of Capital and Income*. San Diego: Simon Publications, 1906.

Gleeson-White, Jane. *Six Capitals, or Can Accountants Save the Planet?* New York: W. W. Norton & Company, 2015.

Gleeson-White, Jane. *Double Entry: How the Merchants of Venice Created Modern Finance*. New York: W. W. Norton & Company, 2012.

Hall, Everett W. *Our Knowledge of Fact and Value*. Chapel Hill: University of North Carolina Press, 1961.

Holland, John H. *Hidden Order: How Adaptation Builds Complexity*. Reading, MA: Perseus Books, 1995.

Inglehart, Ronald, and Christian Welzel. *Modernization, Cultural Change, and Democracy: The Human Development Sequence*. Cambridge, UK: Cambridge University Press, 2005.

Kant, Immanuel. *Groundwork of the Metaphysic of Morals*. Translated by T. K. Abbott. Lexington, KY: BN Publishing, 2010.

Marshall, Alfred. *Principles of Economics*. London: Macmillan and Co., 1890.

McElroy, Mark W. *Social Footprints: Measuring the Social Sustainability Performance of Organizations* (PhD diss.). Groningen, The Netherlands: University of Groningen, 2008.

McElroy, Mark W. *The New Knowledge Management: Complexity, Learning, and Sustainable Innovation*. Burlington, MA: Butterworth-Heinemann, 2003.

McElroy, Mark W., and Martin P. Thomas. "The MultiCapital Scorecard." *Sustainability Accounting Management and Policy Journal* 6, no. 3 (2015): 425–438.

McElroy, Mark W., and Jo M. L. van Engelen. *Corporate Sustainability Management: The Art and Science of Managing Non-Financial Performance*. London: Routledge, 2012.

Meadows, Donella H. *Indicators and Information Systems for Sustainable Development*. Hartland, VT: The Sustainability Institute (Donella Meadows Institute), 1998, accessed March 25, 2016, http://donellameadows.org/wp-content/userfiles/IndicatorsInformation.pdf.

Meadows, Donella H., Dennis L. Meadows, Jorgen Randers, and William W. Behrens, III. *The Limits to Growth*. New York: New American Library, 1972.

Notturno, Mark A. *Science and the Open Society: The Future of Karl Popper's Philosophy*. Budapest: Central European University Press, 2005.

Pacioli, Luca. *Summa de Arithmetica, Geometria, Proportione et Proportionalità*. Venice: Paganino de Paganini, 1494.

Popper, Karl R. *Objective Knowledge—An Evolutionary Approach*. Oxford: Oxford University Press, 1972.

Popper, Karl R. *Logic of Scientific Discovery*. New York: Basic Books, 1959.

Popper, Karl R. *Conjectures and Refutations*. New York: Basic Books, 1962.

Porritt, Jonathon. *Capitalism as if the World Matters*. London: Earthscan, 2005.

Rawls, John. *A Theory of Justice*. Cambridge, MA: Harvard University Press, 1971.

Ringland, Gill, Oliver Sparrow, and Patricia Lustig. *Beyond Crisis: Achieving Renewal in a Turbulent World*. Chichester, West Sussex: John Wiley and Sons, 2010.

Solomons, David. *Divisional Performance Measurement and Control*. New York: Financial Executives Research Foundation, 1965.

Stiglitz, Joseph E., Amartya Sen, and Jean-Paul Fitoussi. *Mis-Measuring Our Lives: Why GDP Doesn't Add Up*. New York: The New Press, 2010.

Stone, Christopher D. "Should Trees Have Standing—Toward Legal Rights for Natural Objects." *Southern California Law Review* 45 (1972): 450–487.

Bibliography

Thomas, Martin P. "Performance That Lasts: How Leading Organisations Measure Performance in 2050." In *New Eyes: The Human Side of Leadership*, eds. Joanne Flinn, Roberto Saco, Mike Staresinic, and Dan Ballbach (London: The Change Leaders, 2013).

Thomas, Martin P. "Scenarios towards Social Dialogue." In *Business Planning for Turbulent Times*, eds. Rafael Ramirez, John W. Selsky, and Kees van der Heijden (London: Earthscan, 2008).

United Nations Environment Programme (UNEP). *Raising the Bar—Advancing Environmental Disclosure in Sustainability Reporting*. Paris: UNEP, 2015.

Vickers, Geoffrey. *The Art of Judgment: A Study of Policy Making*. London: Chapman & Hall, 1965.

von Carlowitz, Hans Carl. *Sylvicultura Oeconomica*. Leipzig: Johann Friedrich Brauns, 1713.

Wackernagel, Mathis, and William Rees. *Our Ecological Footprint: Reducing Human Impact on the Earth*. Gabriola Island, BC, Canada: New Society Publishers, 1996.

INDEX

Note: Page numbers in *italics* refer to figures; page numbers followed by *t* refer to tables.

Index

Index

eBay, 26
Eccles, Robert, 148, 154–56, 157–59
ecological footprint, 1, *13*, 201
economic allocations, 206–7, 208
economic capital. *See also* financial capitals
  accounting adjustments for maintenance of, 211–12
  Context-Based Sustainability lack of considering, 36
  defined, 35
  tangible vs. intangible assets, 135–37, *136*
  as vital capital, 8
economic profit, 62
economic value added, 63, 206
The Economist (journal), 138
ecosystems services, 34
Edwards, Edgar, 62
effective liquidity, 68, 70
E. I. DuPont, 26
Eli Lilly, 26
Emery, Fred E., 161, 179
Emmanuel, Clive, 62
Enforcement rule of Sustainability Code, 189
environmental and social foundation for MultiCapital Scorecard, 12–13, *13*
environmental capital. *See* natural capital
environmental profit and loss accounts (E P&L), 214–15
Environmental Responsibility Reports (Apple), 25–26
E P&L (environmental profit and loss accounts), 214–15
epistemic inclusiveness, 186
epistemology, as variable in sustainability, 183–84, 189–191. *See also* Sustainability Code, the
equity capital
  in capital structure, 59, 61–63, 65–66
  as common metric in case study, 109
  consolidated annual integrated performance worksheets, 110–19*t*
  consolidated group summary, 120, 120–21*t*
  cost of, 60, 62
equity holders
  in noncommercial organizations, 70–72
  as stakeholders, 61–63, 64, 65
equity report (case study), 88–89, 88*t*, *89*

ethics-based metrics, 200. *See also* context-based metrics
explicit transparency of management information, 3, 41
external assurance
  importance of, 167–170, 178
  overview, 147
  valuation of brands, 138–39, 141
external economic capital, 35. *See also* economic capital; financial capitals
externalities
  accounting adjustments for, 214–15
  internalization of, 187
external reporting, 19

facilitating structure, *193*, 194, 196, 197
fact-based metrics, 200. *See also* context-based metrics
Fact / Value rule of Sustainability Code, 188
fair, just, and proportionate allocations, 8, 10, 46, 204–7, 208, 209
Fair Comparison rule of Sustainability Code, 186
Fallibility rule of Sustainability Code, 185
feed forward benefits of MultiCapital Scorecard, 39
financial accounting
  accounting adjustments, 63, 64, 67, 210–15
  focus on tangible assets, 135–36
  as inspiration for MultiCapital Scorecard, 10–11
  valuation of brands, 137–38, 139, 142–43
financial accounts, 63
financial capitals, 59–72. *See also* economic capital
  accounting adjustments for maintenance of, 211–12
  capital structure concerns, 59–61
  debt component of, 59, 63–64, 64*t*
  as economic capital, 35
  equity component of, 59, 61–63
  integrated reporting focus on, 151, 158, 160, 161
  liquidity concerns, 67–70
  MultiCapital Scorecard practice for, 64–72, 66*t*
  real terms residual income, 65–67, 69
financial performance, in MultiCapital Scorecard, 8–9, 33, 36, 64–72, 66*t*

Index

Index

Index

ABOUT THE AUTHORS

Martin P. Thomas, MA, MSc, FCMA, FCIS, CGMA

Castle Studio, Guildford

Martin Thomas is a co-founding principal of Thomas & McElroy LLC. He came to sustainability thinking after completing his MSc in consulting and coaching for change and chairing the Change Leaders. In his thirty-four years at Unilever, he headed Unilever's global strategic planning activities and then had responsibility for several mergers, acquisitions, disposals, and international ventures in various countries at different times. His work was international, mainly at subsidiary executive board level, conducted in four languages and living consecutively on four continents. Since 1999 he has been consulting as call4change and has taken on interim management assignments in various organizations.

Martin's publications include chapters on "Scenarios in Venezuela," in *Business Planning for Turbulent Times* (Earthscan, 2008), written by members of the Oxford Futures Forum, and on "Performance that Lasts" in *New Eyes* (The Change Leaders, 2013).

His focus on measuring organizational performance toward sustainable futures started in 2007 when he decided to complement the activities of the Change Leaders' colleagues in New Angles by operationalizing triple bottom line concepts.

While presenting to the Centre for Social and Environmental Accounting Research at St. Andrews, Martin linked up with *The MultiCapital Scorecard* co-author Mark McElroy. Since 2011, they have been extending Context-Based Sustainability principles and practices to include financials and measure progression toward full sustainability.

Mark W. McElroy, PhD

Mark McElroy is a co-founding principal of Thomas & McElroy LLC. He is an accomplished innovator, consultant, author, and educator in the theory and practice of corporate sustainability management. He is the founder and executive director of the Center for Sustainable Organizations in Vermont and is particularly well known for his development of Context-Based Sustainability, an approach to sustainability measurement, management, and reporting in which performance is seen as a function of what an organization's impacts are or ought to be on vital capitals.

McElroy is also a longtime veteran of management consulting, having spent much of his career at Price Waterhouse, KPMG Peat Marwick—where as a partner he led a national practice—and IBM Consulting. More recently, he created and led Deloitte Consulting's Center for Sustainability Performance in Boston, Massachusetts, a think tank dedicated to the study of sustainability measurement, management, and reporting that he founded.

McElroy earned his PhD in economics and business from the University of Groningen in The Netherlands in 2008, and currently teaches sustainability theory and practice in the MBA in Managing for Sustainability program at Marlboro College in Vermont. He is board chair emeritus at the Donella Meadows Institute, also in Vermont, where he continues to serve on the advisory board.

With Martin Thomas, he is co-creator of the MultiCapital Scorecard. Their joint articles have appeared in *Sustainability Accounting, Management and Policy Journal, The World Financial Review,* and the *Harvard Business Review.*

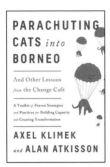

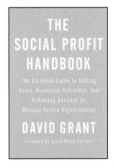